Blind Vision
VOLUME I

WE HOLD
THESE
TRUTHS

CURTIS C. GRECO

Advantage®

Published by Advantage, Charleston, South Carolina.
Member of Advantage Media Group.

ADVANTAGE is a registered trademark and the Advantage colophon is a trademark of Advantage Media Group, Inc.

Printed in the United States of America.

ISBN: 978-1-59932-169-1
LCCN: 2009912522

This publication is designed to provide accurate and authoritative information in regard to the subject matter covered. It is sold with the understanding that the publisher is not engaged in rendering legal, accounting, or other professional services. If legal advice or other expert assistance is required, the services of a competent professional person should be sought.

Most Advantage Media Group titles are available at special quantity discounts for bulk purchases for sales promotions, premiums, fund raising, and educational use. Special versions or book excerpts can also be created to fit specific needs.

For more information, please write: Special Markets, Advantage Media Group, P.O. Box 272, Charleston, SC 29402 or call 1.866.775.1696.

Visit us online at **advantagefamily**.com

"*Democracy and professional sports have one big thing in common: At the end of the day, sniping at your opponent is not the same as being the best and winning the game. Nobody does a better job than Curtis Greco of illustrating the power and beauty of democracy, and showing readers how living and thriving in a democracy is a team sport that involves playing the game instead of sitting back and doing all that partisan sniping that's tearing our country apart. America's one team, and Curtis Greco makes a great coach.*"

—PAT WILLIAMS, SENIOR VICE PRESIDENT, ORLANDO MAGIC,
AUTHOR OF *NAIL IT!* & *DALY WISDOM*

"*Greco is the megaphone from which our founding fathers are screaming 'please stop this madness'. We have fumbled, bumbled, and stumbled off the path that they struggled to secure. The scary truth is that the attack on human freedoms is no longer a frontal assault, but a peripheral anesthetic experience in which we are both the criminal and the victim. Greco's words awaken us to the fact that with every ambivalent shrug of our shoulders (and with every free hand-out from the government) the noose tightens around our neck and removes a cornerstone from our true personal and collective purpose. Greco's book captures a truth that would have to seem surreal to the likes of Thomas Jefferson and an aberration to Benjamin Franklin. Finally, as we are exhausted from the reality of Greco's words, he provides us with good news!!! TODAY, only in America could the ceiling on any one person's greatness be his or her willingness to work harder and smarter. We will have to 'engage' with our mind and spirit to keep it possible for us to 'have life, liberty and the pursuit of happiness'. Every American should read this book!*"

—TODD ZAUGG, PRINCIPAL & FOUNDER, MATRIX ACHIEVEMENT
GROUP, LLC, AUTHOR, *WARRIOR SALES MONK*

"In Curtis Greco's new book We Hold These Truths…, *you'll find out why having the right to vote is just the beginning, and why organizations who promote voter education and engagement are so important for preserving the bedrock of what makes America great for generations to come."*

—CHRISSY FAESSEN, ROCK THE VOTE

DEDICATION

"...we mutually pledge to each other our Lives,
our Fortunes, and our sacred Honor."

To the Love of a Wife, my Children, a Father, a Mother,
a Brother, many Sisters, Uncles, Aunts & Cousins!

To "Americans," the world over! This "Series," is my Gift to you!

But most of all,

To an Infinite & Perfect Love, binding one and all,
from whom "meaning & form" finds its cause!

Blind Vision

NOT SO LONG AGO I had the occasion to sit and visit with my father. At that time, he had progressed well into his 80's and though time had waged a battle with his body, his mind was as crisp as ever. I asked his opinion about the times we are living in and what he observed, over the years, to be the most significant changes. I was amazed by what he said.

- "People, at their core, never really change. However, I have noticed that we seem to have moved away from them [core values]."

- "Despite what history may say, people were not happy about what Roosevelt was doing...it's not all that different from what I see happening today."

- "If there had been the same media exposure of global affairs in the 30's and 40's, Pearl Harbor would never have happened and the American people would have felt much different about the war and Roosevelt would never have been elected."

- "This technology thing – yes, information is more easily obtained, but I think it has pushed people into being more detached and ambivalent."

- "But the thing I've noticed most is that people seem to have lost their sense of common purpose."

If I were to add anything to his comments, I would say the abstract notion of consequence has been degraded and seems to be fading on toward oblivion. We have become desensitized not only to the impact our choices have on our own lives, but perhaps equally important, the impact our choices have on others. This series takes an overview of fiscal interests and policy, not only of the United States, but also of the world, and further examines the financial and social consequences of those very policies. However, I believe the most critical perspective from which to view these issues is through the lens of freedom and the definitive critique of what constitutes the expressions of, or impediments to, liberty.

In one sense, the series may be seen as a *call to action*, in another respect, it may be viewed as a "political and economic retrospective." At best, it may even be both.

To illustrate and underscore this body of work and my own observations and conclusions, I have drawn on a few of my favorite historical figures, such as Thomas Jefferson, Benjamin Franklin, Andrew Jackson, and Don Miguel de Cervantes, to name a few.

A final note on the series title, *Blind Vision*. I appreciate the use of words, in combination, to paint a mental picture from which to convey a message. Let me explain further: Many years ago, I lost an older sister to a congenital heart disorder. Today, modern medicine would likely have saved her; however, it was a different time. Her name was Cynthia – to me though, she was simply known as Cindy. In addition to her heart condition, she was also blind, though she had so well adapted, one would never have known.

As one of 10 children, I am positioned in the younger half of the regiment and occasionally Cindy would be assigned the task of minding a few of the younger group. I was always amazed, no, I was stunned by how she managed to know what sort of trouble I was brewing and her proficiency in interfering with most of my misadventures. I can still, to this very day, clearly hear her voice: "Curtis!"

I recall asking her, "How do you do it?" and she replied, "I'm blind, but I can still see what I know!" Many years would pass and this moment, like others before or since, resolved to memory storage until June of 2008. I had just concluded a talk with a group. A few folks approached me and we began a spirited exchange. As I recall it, I found myself responding to one of the questions with something like this: "Look, even if you were blind, your mind's eye will image what you know to be true!" Instantly, I saw the face of my sister Cindy and I heard her voice once again.

The most compelling reason for this series is my personal love for the ideals that inspired the creation of this country's form of government: "Life, Liberty and the Pursuit of Happiness!" I believe that man's greatest and ultimate challenge is to perfect the means to void his divisive tendencies. Each is called to express ones own unique gift which, in the process of our expressing, defines ones very purpose. However, a gift, by its very nature, can only be expressed in the physical realm and with the rhythm of action, and so, express it we must!

This gift must and will only ever occur freely and with unfettered interchange accompanied by the reward which, I believe, will inevitably come when all engage in the same pursuit. We must move smartly to perfect these ideals and overcome all impediments to its accomplishment. One might even say it is our collective "calling." There is no other place to go; the time is now and the place is right where one finds him or herself to be!

Once I accepted the challenge of actually taking on the project, I found myself wondering if what you are about to read is necessarily new. The manner in which I present the message may be novel and you may even find my own personal comments poetically enticing. However, the fact of the matter is, no matter how well scripted the message may be, we truly do already know the "core values!" I believe God has planted these seeds of truths and they are forever resident in one's mind and soul. They are what you intuitively know to be true.

How then does the idea relate to this three-part series? A fair question. The most efficient way to explain it might best be in the form of an allegory. For instance: A man is walking down the street on his way to work. Summer, winter, rain, snow or shine, year after year, he walks the same course day after day. Some days he gives and some days he receives but always what he carries is a function of what he collects from one place or another. Even without speaking, you know what he does for a living, don't you? Yes, of course you do. The markings are in the images your mind forms from the verbal cues of this simple story. Yes indeed, he's a postman. Simple enough!

Yes, of course the confusion of the day is marked by many indicators of truth sandwiched between the clutter of newspaper articles, five-second sound-bites, talk radio, non-stop breaking news, well crafted speeches and emails. Yet despite the confusion of mixed messages, the markings of what is "true" is found in our conscience which surfaces to filter the input. What we discover from this filtering process is the dissonance between what we observe and what we know, intuitively, to be true. All one is left with is a discordant sense of disbelief which is most conspicuously identified when one finds him or herself uttering: "Who do they think they're kidding?" Well, *they* think it's you!

I, like many, find myself more and more disenfranchised from a political system that bears no resemblance to the promise of our national heritage. Our national sovereignty and economic future has been repackaged and out-sourced with the speed and efficiency of an IRS tax lien; entire industries have been relocated, leaving behind vacant warehouses, silent factories, idle resources of all types and worst of all, broken dreams.

In a country whose very identity rests upon the genius of an ideal that prior to its formation had never seen the light of day, seeing the promise of this land and the industry of so vibrant and genuine a people summarily laid to waste is, as it is for most, simply heart breaking! And then of course are our children, I think of my own and I ask myself: "How can we let this stand?" I hear others say, "What has happened?" I hear even more say, "Somebody's got to do something about this!" And when I hear this comment, I often think of the following story which I heard some years ago. Perhaps one day I'll share the story of how I came to hear it.

It's a story about a man who walks in to a church. You see, he's down on his luck; he's lost his business, he's lost his family and his view of the world is hopeless and in complete disarray. He walks up to the altar and stares squarely at the image upon the cross and with the strained voice of a person in emotional and physical pain he attempts to impale the image with his words. "Why? Why have you done this to me? Why have you let the world fall upon me this way? The world is in turmoil and you sit idly by and just let it happen! What kind of love is this you speak of? How can you speak to me of goodness when this is to be the world in which a man finds himself? Why, oh why, don't you do something?" His energy spent, the room's light gently softens and becomes suddenly still. And then, awakening the stillness of the moment is the warmth of a soft resonant voice and it speaks these simple words: "I did; I sent you."

I'll ask of you this: Please do remember, in particular, the last five words of the preceding paragraph. They are a foundation on which to build a remarkable life!

And so, there it is, the overall message. Read it, enjoy it and be inspired by its message.

BLIND VISION

"I'VE NO NEED FOR VISION TO SEE WHAT I KNOW TO BE TRUE."

CURTIS C. GRECO, JUNE 2009

FOREWORD

ON JANUARY 10 IN PHILADELPHIA, a concerned citizen published a short monograph that brought into perspective all that men like him believed and held dear. The year was 1776, the document was called *Common Sense,* and the writer was a man named Thomas Payne, newly arrived in America.

Common Sense was not a large book. But it carried a very important message. Payne wrote it, he said, because, "The cause of America is, in a great measure, the cause of all mankind."

Now, nearly two and a half centuries later, a concerned citizen named Curtis Greco has written a reminder that Payne's first message is still a message to be remembered, and that the cause of America still matters to the world.

We Hold These Truths ... is the first volume in the new *Blind Vision* series of political and historical commentaries by Greco. They are an intensely personal examination of the ideals that inspired and shaped our government. But they are more than that. They are also a clear-eyed analysis of where and how those ideals have been subverted and distorted – and where they threaten to come loose.

In this book are answers to questions like these:

> How did we come to have a government that uses conflict to disguise an essentially undemocratic agenda?

> What are the true economic implications of globalism?

> What are the social implications of wealth redistribution through excessive taxation and broadened entitlements?

What are the legal implications of open borders and unimpeded illegal immigration?

These questions seem familiar because they are the questions we have all asked ourselves and our neighbors. We need answers to them, and this little book provides them. By harvesting the wisdom of his favorite historical figures, including Thomas Jefferson, Curtis Greco shows us how to find the truths that have always been with us.

This is not a large book. But in its important message is the power and clarity to do for America today what Thomas Payne did for Americans so long ago. It will help us all discover the value and importance of simple common sense.

—AUSTIN HILL, Columnist, Talk Show Host, Author, *The Virtues of Capitalism: A Moral Case For Free Markets*

Contents

A Note from the Author

NOT ENOUGH IS SAID about critical moments in one's life. We often conceal these for various reasons though most often it is more likely that we think, "Oh, we'll get around to it!" or, "Ah, well, I'd better keep it to myself, no one will believe it!" This, however, is not one of those instances. I deliberately intend for all who read these works to know of a specific critical moment and the gratitude I hold in my heart for those who are integral to it. First, the entire staff at Advantage Media Group, an extraordinary group of talented individuals whose assembly is a monument to the truly remarkable vision of Adam Witty, an extraordinary man!

Vision can only ever truly be inspiring if, as its architect, there is an individual capable of its mastery. In Volumes I, II, and III of the *Blind Vision* series, I introduce The Imperfect Messenger Foundation and I fully intend for it to become an iconic resource through which I and others disseminate thought provoking work. And yes, the material you have in hand is indeed the product of my efforts. However, the form you will soon view received its first breath of life from the inspired vision of Denis Boyles, AMG's Senior Editor to whom I will be eternally grateful! For me, mastery is only ever known when combined with action: Editor Priscilla Turner is the archetypical form of this ideal and has demonstrated it so lovingly through her guidance, precision and elegant refinements. From where I started, even I could never have imagined the result and I will look forward to working with her again and again.

To say that I have saved the *best for last* would not be fair to those I've mentioned thus far, so perhaps it is more appropriate for me to express my intention this way: I've saved the most dear for last! Gregg Stebben is an exceptionally gifted gentlemen. I've known him since I was 15 years old and although we accompanied events and careers which led us on separate paths for much of this time, a wondrous fate brought us back together. For this, I've only to express a hearty thanks to his marvelous brother, Marty. To the point: It is not an overstatement to say that none of what is before you would appear the way it does were it not for Gregg. He possesses a unique self-effacing form of warmth and gentleness that is supremely magnetic. He is an accomplished writer and media presence and most importantly, he is truly a good man in every sense of the word. I do my best to express regard and admiration for him at every possible opportunity.

And so you ask: *What is the critical moment?* Consider, if you will, thinking of life as a canvas upon which each of us records and expresses our own unique and individual gift in a color and by a stroke uniquely our own. Not one stroke may be omitted, not one expression missed or unrecorded — to do so would forever change the image and then for all time it would remain incomplete. For me, the *critical moment* for this endeavor is this: That at one moment in time I should be so blessed to have such magnificent talent expressing their gift upon my canvas! To omit just one would have made the outcome something different, something less! They have given me an extraordinary gift which I now present to you the Reader and I do believe we owe each other our very best effort. I couldn't possibly imagine a more perfect way to paint a life in color!

A Perspective

THE COMMON THREAD that binds one man to another is the ideals and understandings they hold in common. The measure, more or less, of the success of that interaction is also the extent to which the product of the same resonates from a fundamental truth. I can find no document that so universally refines a fundamental cause, so perfectly expressing a foundational thread upon which all will find a firm footing, than the magnificently crafted Declaration of Independence. Thomas Jefferson masterfully defines, for all time, the gateway of unalienable potential; the fertile ground from which all rights to the fruits of ones' *providential form* is professed as unassailable. This documents preamble is truly remarkable:

> *"We hold these truths to be **self-evident**, that **all men are created equal**, that they are endowed by their **Creator** with certain **unalienable Rights**, that among these are **Life, Liberty and the pursuit of Happiness**. That to secure these rights, Governments are instituted among Men, deriving their just powers from the **consent of the governed**, That whenever any Form of Government becomes destructive of these ends, it is the **Right of the People to alter or to abolish it,...**"*

Scholars far better equipped than I are free to express a far more collegiate disquisition as to the historical significance of the document and the many influences from which Mr. Jefferson drew while engaged in this efforts however, for now let me just highlight a few personal observations which I find most powerful.

In his writing he identifies fundamental truths that until that time, though frequently mused by many, never appeared as a foundation for a form of government. Terms such as "self-evident," "created equal," "endowed by their Creator," "unalienable rights," "consent of the governed," and "the right of the People to alter or to abolish it" not only suggest a profound understanding of providential ideals and yet, simultaneously they are inexorably linked to one another so fundamentally that without one the whole becomes imperfect. Lastly and perhaps most inspired, he makes no suggestion that these are newly discovered nor does he suggest that they are dispensed by some legislated act or dispensation. Oh no these are not of man at all but from a source far more omniscient.[1]

"TRANSFIXED BY THE WONDER OF THE STAR FIELD DARKNESS OF INFINITE SPACE, I PONDERED THE ORIGINS OF MAN HIS NATURE AND LIMITS. SILENTLY REFLECTING ITS IMAGE UPON ME I WAS TO HEAR THE WORD: INFINITE!"[2]

I begin here not as an introduction to a discussion of American history but as point of reference for what I hope to accomplish in this composition. For various reasons this country has set out on a political and economic course that has, I believe, lead the nation and its people away from its founding principles. Consequently we now question these very principles as well as our system of government. Further, it is my observation that it is neither our founding principles nor our system of government that is the problem. The problem IS the *practices* of government

---

1   Throughout the entirety of this material I will use the word "Foundation" and "Fundamental Principles" frequently. When you happen upon these words, I trust you will recall this entry.

2   Insertions, in visual presentation form such as in this instance, appear throughout this composition with no reference to its author. Their source, be it various compositions or public presentation, is the product of my own efforts and/or authorship.

which no longer seems willing or able to operate by its specific mandate and in the service of the "consent of the governed." It is the practice of distortion that has and continues to affect our standing amongst ourselves and as a nation in the global community. These foundations I speak of are universal to all and if we intend to espouse their ideals then I would suggest that we first refine these in the function(s) of our own process and leave others (nations) to perfect their own. Then, and if only on their own, they should discover our approach worth replicating, they might express their individual desire to make our success theirs as well. Lastly, I hope to present throughout, albeit in deliberately rudimentary terms, economic, monetary and political points all from both an historical and contemporary perspective which, ultimately, will conclude with my final presentation, *Volume III: Valor in Prosperity*. This particular volume contains a summary resolution entitled *A Functional Stimulus*, a composition which is, to be sure, a must read!

I readily admit there are men and women of *letters* who may engage in theoretical discourse on these subjects to a degree that will draw the very air from your lungs, which again, is duly noted. However, I intend not to offend their knowledge base with a simpleton's offering however I will assert that my faith, my formal, private and practical education along with my years engaged in successfully generating income from which I provide comfort and care to my family (all, by the way, without government assistance and despite government interference) make me eminently qualified to discourse soundly on these matters. I've seen both the practice of success and the markers of failure and as is the case with our foundations, they are absolute and most certainly NOT theoretical. I make none nor do I offer any apologies for the product of my cumulative experience and the historical compass on which they are based and neither should you.

I believe it equally important to note that I'm not, as you will soon see, a patron of any particular political party. In other words, the only dog I have in this hunt is uniquely an American one, accordingly, I find discussion about *party* wholly irrelevant. With this thought in mind and observing the political pandering of the day, *it is clear to say both parties are equally at fault, both possessing an equal measure if toxic guile the consequence of which is the near complete reprogramming of a proud political and economic heritage.* We no longer espouse the value of productive capability, we now champion the pirate! Where once there was an ideology of republicanism[3], we now rally around the proven fallacies of collectivism. The valor of the common man, once sacred and protected, is now profane and proletariat. Perhaps the image I intend is best characterized by the image of the helpless vagrant begging at the gate of his lord and master, *feed me!* The *ism* of the day is now a particularly malignant form of elitism — a hegemonic cabal of pelegian misfits who through a form of philosophical nepotism have transformed an entire culture. What we now have at the helm of government is, in effect, a heretical and misanthropic form of self-entitled elites!

I agree that many who read these words may label them dramatic and profane, however equal only to my right to say (or print) them, is your right to disagree with my perspective. This right is expressly preserved by way of the First Amendment (the first of ten Amendments known as the *Bill of Rights*) to the Constitution of the United States yet NO WHERE in the Constitution do I see the document specify party or partisanship or, for that matter, as an enumerated power and never have I seen any principle of our foundation assigned either to one or

---

3   Republicanism: Ironically, this term refers to a "representative form of government" and not a political party. Democracy, is only the process.

the other (party). Further, if one were to review James Madison's essay *Federalist No. 10*, which is a component of the *Federalist Papers* series, one will witness first hand the concern of the founding father as to the evils of partisan politics. Abusing the privilege of office with the overbite of partisanship, just to name but one, is shameful and disruptive. These practiced excesses are abhorrent and constitute a breach of public trust which are lasting and detrimental to all far beyond the measure of personal gain and party affiliation. It is, after all, the UNITED States of America!

The Constitution of the United States, for all intents and purposes, IS a living document born out of the revolutionary quest to claim the inveterate right of self-determination. It is not, nor will it ever be, an evolutionary document. *Why*, you might ask? Simply and to the point; the foundations upon which it rests are timeless, unchanging and unwavering! Natural Law is as old as time and likewise completely unaffected by the passing fancies of the human condition or mind. Yes, we have refined the document to resolve and/or perfect, particularly in the case of the 13th Amendment (the abolition of slavery), select issues, however, it is important to note that no amendment has yet been added or recanted that has changed the very foundation of the document.

Unfortunately, the far reaching effects of legislating from the bench, also known as *judicial activism*, have introduced a very dangerous trend where courts have vacated the "will of the people" in a most egregious and recalcitrant manner. It was never the intention of the enabling document to invite the courts to legislate through supervenient interpretations which are and have become an illusory and completely manufactured practice. It must be the practice of the judiciary/courts to be only an extension of the overriding intent of the Constitution, as "...the supreme law of the land." which must be uniformly applied and not by interpretation or by syllogism — both of which are colored by the bias of perspective. Government, or in this case the courts, will, when left to their own impulses, craft means which only serve to mandate their very existence and always at the cost of your inalienable rights. It is from these practices the dangerously divisive notion of the "evolutionary" practice of discretionary governance appears and soils the light and brilliance of representative government.

"TO PERFECT WHAT EXISTS BETWEEN THE CREATED
GOVERNMENT AND THE CONSENTING GOVERNED IS THE IMPLICIT
UNDERSTANDING THAT THE SOCIAL CONTRACT MADE BETWEEN
THEM MUST BE RIGOROUSLY HONORED! AS A NATION, THE
SUCCESS OF ALL OUR MOST NOBLE PURSUITS IS MEASURED BY
THE ABSOLUTE INTEGRITY OF THIS CONTRACT IN ACTION."

With respect to the span of recorded human history, this nation and the foundation on which it stands, to be sure, is quite young and continues the struggle toward perfection. Not only with the principles that lie back of and are integral to the ideal simply and yet profoundly defined as *freedom*, but the vigilance required to pursue it with complete and unwavering insistence. Abraham Lincoln assembled the words of his *Gettysburg Address* artfully and from a keen sense and understanding of the collective and universal conscience of man that from the dawn of time has been our innate sense of destiny. We witness in his words, brought by pen (or quill) to paper in a time of great struggle, that which possess a sensed devotion resonating with an impassioned plea! With deference to Mr. Lincoln's mastery I include the entire text here however, I have taken the liberty of underlining passages to which I would encourage the reader to pay particular attention:

> *"Four score and seven years ago our fathers brought forth on this continent a new nation, conceived in Liberty, and dedicated to the proposition that <u>all men are created equal</u>.*
>
> *Now we are engaged in a great civil war, testing whether that nation, or any nation, so conceived and so dedicated, can long endure. We are met on a great battlefield of that war. We have come to dedicate a portion of that field, as a final resting place for those who here gave their lives that that nation might live. It is altogether fitting and proper that we should do this.*
>
> *But, in a larger sense, we can not dedicate—we can not consecrate—we can not hallow—this ground. The brave men, living and dead, who struggled here, have consecrated it, far above our poor power to add or detract. The world will little note, nor long remember what we say here, but it can never forget what they did here. <u>It is for us the living, rather, to be dedicated here to the unfinished work which they who fought here have thus far so nobly advanced. It is rather for us to be here dedicated to the great task remaining before us</u>—that from these honored dead we take increased devotion to that cause for which they gave the last full measure of devotion—<u>that we here highly resolve that these dead shall not have died in vain—that this nation, under God, shall have a new birth of freedom—and that government: of the people, by the people, for the people, shall not perish from the earth.</u>"*

I believe that as a people, in the quest to insist on and master these providential ideals, we MUST never aspire to anything less. If we remain steadfast for one another to so worthy a cause, one day, the people may yet celebrate its common reward!

As you the reader make your way through this exposé kindly keep the following thought ever present in your thinking: it has never been my intention to make a statement as to political affiliations. Keeping in mind the age old axiom of *divide and conquer* and to restate a point made earlier, I find that discussions on or about political affiliation to be nothing more than wasted exercise. I also find that the distinction of political affiliation to be nothing more than a political banner of interests adverse to the true principles of freedom - just barely concealing their true intent.

As the years have passed I've taken great interest in the inquiry of people of various political affiliations and I find little difference at the core of their ambitions. They simply want to be *free* to *do*! The issue then, ultimately, comes to the question of how is one to be truly free? This question appears in two fundamental forms which are, at their core, polar opposites. They resolve, fundamentally, as follows:

- Is freedom pursued by the individual unobstructed by government?

Or,

- Is freedom pursued only through the use of governance?

I will not attempt to conceal my personal beliefs from the reader as I personally would find that completely disingenuous, accordingly, I believe that the only good government is a limited one and I believe within that limited form the primary purpose of which is (only) to guard the freedoms and well-being of the people who grant the very existence of said government. To believe that one's freedoms can be given *in trust* to an entity in exchange for an undisclosed outcome is to place a infinite degree of trust in a system that is incapable of comprehending the *treasure* which has been placed in and simultaneously defined as said *trust*. The risk of this is to grant what then becomes a cumulative barrier, which inevitably renders those very freedoms unrecoverable, retrievable only through contest. After all,

"FREEDOM, ONCE SURRENDERED, IS FREEDOM LOST!"

I believe that over time we can observe what happens when government is permitted to morph beyond the limited role of good government. No hyperbole, no well-crafted speech, no political or media bias can mask this truth. If the soundness of this statement is not presently a resident of your conspicuous thoughts one is soon to discover, in the material presented throughout this entire *series*, sufficient evidence to support the fundamental truth that not only does government regularly operate beyond its prescribed limits, it actually operates in a manner specifically designed to assure its ability to do so!

To be fair, I acknowledge those among us who feel it is the role of government to provide for one's freedom by passing various forms of beneficial or benevolent legislation. Holding to this belief is to suggest that government has the means of its own and from its own resources the product it purports to be able to deliver. Sadly, this belief has been effectively institutionalized in the conscience of the people, not only in this country, but in many others throughout the world. To get straight to the point: Government has NO SUCH MEANS as it has no industry of its own from which it can manufacture or generate the wealth/benefits it intends to distribute. Those that believe that the government can do so need to understand and fully adopt this *basic truth*:

> "WHAT ONE THINKS GOVERNMENT HAS TO GIVE
> MUST FIRST UNDERSTAND IT ACCUMULATES ONLY
> BY TAKING! IT OCCURS NO OTHER WAY!"

So then we are left with one final question: Is it just to take from one that which is theirs by birthright or through the product of their industry? Further, is the concept of freedom enhanced by instituting the practices of those whose philosophy allows them to believe they can? There is a great crisis of government and it revolves simply on the substance and essence of these very questions. As a nation, the great cause of our time is to claim the appropriate answer. As you read through the product of my effort this question, in various forms as well as related substance, will appear with deliberate regularity.

Before moving on, I can think of no better way to present *a point of departure* toward the discourse that follows than to offer an appropriate quote or two:

> "*...a government big enough to supply you with everything you need, is a government big enough to take everything you have...*"[4]

> "VIGILANCE HAS NO LIMITS IN ITS PRESERVATION OF FREEDOM!"

---

4   It has long been my understanding that this was a Thomas Jefferson quote. However, I've not been able to verify this with absolute certainty. It may very well be a variation of a comment by/from former President Gerald R. Ford. Regardless, the truth of it belongs to the certainty of fact.

This statement is particularly absolute when applied to the defense of one's freedoms from the impositions of an obsessive and intrusive tyrant! And then of course there are the passionate expressions of Thomas Jefferson, circa 1811:

> *"When we reflect that the eyes of the virtuous all over the earth are turned with anxiety on us as the only depositories of the sacred fire of liberty, and that our falling into anarchy would decide forever the destinies of mankind and seal the political heresy that man is incapable of self-government, the only contest between divided friends should be who will dare farthest into the ranks of the common enemy."*

Before proceeding, indulge me this: kindly review Mr. Jefferson's words once again.

"...Of Unknown Good"

TRAVELING THE UNITED STATES in your choice of transport is an absolute delight! The contrasts in geography, weather and most importantly, People, are not to be missed. Another interesting note (and this one stood out like an empty field in Nebraska!) occurred a few years ago when my family and I were traveling the country. We made a point to exit the interstate system as frequently as possible driving through the many small towns that *dot* the mid and costal boundaries of the country. What we discovered, first hand, was that Walt Disney's Main Street USA was, most definitely, a reproduction.

The quaint and cozy demeanor of these small towns was absolutely captivating. It seemed as though every *Main Street* we drove through, so long as there wasn't a WalMart in sight, continued to be a thriving *hub* of the community. From the local grocery store to the *Rexall* drug and soda fountain and hardware store, the image was timeless! In one small town, as I recall it was in Indiana, we (even) discovered a flickering neon sign of a *Schwinn* bicycle store. Sadly, like so many iconic brands of Americana, *Schwinn* bicycles are no longer made in the U.S. and the recent offerings, well, they're "Made in China."

Of course, one can quickly reverse this blissful image by taking the dramatic city tour of *rue de rustte* and although these images scar the nation's landscape, our tour of the old *ribbon of industry* traverses Michigan, Ohio and on into Pennsylvania. It is perfectly awful and equally sobering to see hundreds of industrial buildings standing as a monument to progressive industrial decay each with a sobering epitaph that reads something like, *Sorry, but you're not needed any more!* It would seem that the locusts' lust for the cheap and malleable labor pools of Asia was just too strong to find value in keeping and perfecting a good idea.

So much industrial and productive muscle left simply to atrophy, wither and die. A supreme and absolute waste!

What has happened is not just the disintegration of an economic engine but the *scattering to the winds* of an ideal that has been the *bindings* of a Peoples' common bond the effects and consequences of which we will endure for decades to come. If one doubts this, visit for yourself the once vibrant economic centers of this country, the trauma is unmistakable.

I'm of the opinion that it is far more noble and universally beneficial to export a product and the message of freedom; however, we must never auction our *ideals.* In other words: feed a man to fish and he eats for a day. Teach a man to fish and he'll feed himself for life.

The mistake one could make by misinterpreting my comments is to believe in or arrive at a conclusion that suggests a brooding lament or the longing for a once-better time. Not so! One can never relive in the past an inspired vision of the future: The promise of the future, whatever it may be, is the product of inspired thought and exists in form (only) beyond the application of effort.

I suppose an alternative title for this three-part series could very well have been, *A View to the Future from a Perspective of What's Past!* however what I truly intend for you, the reader, is to rediscover the truly unique components of the republican form of government; why it is the ultimate recipe for refining and perfecting mankind's most noble cause and how and by what methods sound governance, when left to the divisiveness of impulse, robustly reconfigures its design and becomes, as we see in our time, so utterly detached and adverse to the causes of Freedom and the Will of the Consenting Governed.

I am less interested in the by *who* and the *what* that has happened and more concerned as to the *Form* that has moved in to replace it! For Americans the world over this should register upon your mind in a manner and sense that should *stir* your curiosity and concern. In the end, we must reclaim not what is lost but more so, that which is LASTING! In the final component of this series, *Volume: III – Valor in Prosperity*, I present a series of conceptual measures that offer specific and practical tools for accomplishing this very task.

Fortunately, as history frequently illustrates, adverse circumstances crumble in the face of a multitude of Individuals armed with forthright purpose and conviction. With this thought in mind, I fully expect that there will be a sufficient number who will find, in the following words, a common bond:

"AN AMERICAN IS NOT ONLY THE INDIVIDUAL WHO MAY FIND ON THESE SHORES A COMPANION IN PROVIDENTIAL IDEALS HOWEVER, IT IS TRULY AND ONLY THESE PROVIDENTIAL IDEALS THAT DEFINE AN AMERICAN! IT IS A PULSE THAT RESONATES WITH THE RHYTHM OF TRUTH IN PEOPLE OF ALL NATIONS WHOSE HEARTS BEAT WITH THE CADENCE OF BUT ONE WORD! FREEDOM! IT IS THEN NOT ONLY FOR THIS UNION TO CHAMPION SO NOBLE A CAUSE BUT FOR ALL TO ASSERT AND ASCEND TO THE IDEAL OF FREEDOM, LIBERTY AND JUSTICE! BY DOING SO, WE BANISH TYRANNY, IN ALL ITS FORMS, TO THE REGIME OF FAILURE!"

The absolute and unwavering commitment to the preservation of freedom must be a constant resident in one's conscious and subconscious thought. I believe this to be so integral to the concept of freedom for it is most certainly true that every manner of inert form evolving from the inspired genius of man gains entry to the realm of life and does so ONLY by way of this portal. One must be free, ABSOLUTELY FREE TO DO AND TO BE! The ideal of freedom is, most definitely, the breath of life for all mankind and so, toward its perfection, nothing in an individual's lifetime matters more! Why? Because...

"WE THE PEOPLE BECOME LABORED BY THE OMISSIONS OF UNKNOWN GOOD INTRUSIVE GOVERNMENT SILENCES!"

Conflict And Selective Ideals

*"I am for a government rigorously frugal and simple ...
I am for free commerce with all nations; political connection with none; and little or no diplomatic establishment."*

"The true theory of our Constitution is surely the wisest and best, that the States are independent as to everything within themselves, and united as to everything respecting foreign nations. Let the General Government be reduced to foreign concerns only, and let our affairs be disentangled from those of all other nations..."

"The happiness and prosperity of our citizens is the only legitimate object of government."

THREE PERFECTLY SUITED QUOTES, each the product of Thomas Jefferson - which I'm certain will come as no surprise. I find his mind so philosophically graceful, so utterly and supremely uncluttered that any man would have the right to covet. I've had these quotes bookmarked for years and from time to time, when revisiting his writings and correspondence, I am drawn to these specific comments for their acuity in precisely illustrating, for me, the clarity of his perspective. On more than one occasion I would find myself pondering this question: How could he have known of the risks and the challenges posterity would (likely) face?

The answer came to me some time later when I overheard a comment having something to do with the Constitution's being an outdated document whose purpose had passed and ought to be relegated to the ash-heap of history. When I heard this comment, the following thought came to mind:

"CONTEMPT IS OFTEN ONLY THE GREAT FEAR OF CONSCIENCE WHOSE IMAGE IS STARING AT YOU IN DISGUST!"

Which is to say; we generally prefer to avoid confrontation with principle particularly when incompatible with our less than noble ambitions. Whatever the case, the point remains this: The answer to my question about Mr. Jefferson's foresight was that it wasn't foresight at all. He knew what the risks were as the very same conflicts that exist now, existed in his time as well. With this realization it became clear that my strongly-held belief or supposition was correct: The Constitution is even more relevant today, particularly because we haven't yet seemed to grasp that as a prescription for sound self-government, how important and near perfect the document actually is. Further, in a time were the aggregation of political and social turmoil, international conflagrations and economic plundering are at pandemic levels, the compass resource offered by the Constitution is even more important than ever before. We must restore ourselves to the understanding that it is ONLY the Constitutional mandate which defines Self-Governance and most certainly NOT Political Bias or Mood. Ironically, what we have seemingly mastered is how *not* to engage in sound governance as it was intended. I'm of the opinion that it's about time we give it a proper go and progress toward — not further away from — this worthy ambition.

In any case I find these three quotes to be among the most refined pre-scription for a national compass should we want to plot a true a course toward a sustainable social, political and/or economic recovery. That is if there is a collective belief that *better* is preferable to "more of less" particularly when the latter suggests that "less" is the outcome of col-lective resignation. Where do you, the reader, stand? You must know, there is no middle ground, there is ONLY one or the other.

I have had the privilege of visiting with a great many people from all walks of life. I've read hundreds of published commentary and the com-monality of their message is clear, the people are completely disgusted with the government's positioning of this nation so perilously close to the cliff. With each new day offering yet another indiscretion by of the ruling class, along with a continuous assault on their conscience, the people are becoming ever more troubled. The very soul of a nation lies in the balance.

Considering the ideal of the republican (representative) form of gov-ernment, it is its nature, its hope, to pursue the noblest course of action for the benefit of all. It is for this reason that when speaking of this ambition we must come to understand that its pursuit is best accom-panied by a command of this ideal. We might even further refine the "ideal" in this manner: that though "all" may not be in equal accord as to how one might individually express his or her freedom, there is however, a majority of will that insists that this liberty is a given, an absolute must! Rest assured,

"THERE IS A GRAVE CONSEQUENCE IN EXCHANGING
MAJORITY OF WILL WITH THE MINORITY OF MOB RULE!"

Mob rule, absent the principles of sound government, is nothing more than an assembly of sociopaths who make good copy (or press) by their bizarre and reckless behavior. They are the conspicuous who champion one political mantra or another and are capable of changing color with the efficiency of a chameleon or the militant activists who pistol-whip public sentiment by threat. These individuals are most definitely not representative of *The People*; they are however, only beings who in their confusion equate the ability to speak and bi-pedal stance with those who pursue rational thought, virtue and character. They are only, to be sure, nothing more than a virus in human form and though the faces and messages may change from day to day, they are none the less predictable in their purpose — not unlike a mechanical wind-up toy or programmable digital voice box.

"No, The People are those who intuitively grasp and understand what the Constitution means and though they may not be able to recite it word for word they recognize, without seeing, what they know to be true and nobly go about their day pursuing it!"

These are *The People* who fuel the economic system with the means necessary for it to function. These are the creative minds, the industrious masses, the possessors of passionate soul who give life to idea and imagination as the absolute product and expression of divinity and their personal industry. These are those who provide the lifeblood of the ideal of freedom and the commerce that peacefully coexists with said ideal. These are the silent and increasingly oppressed. These are the people whose voice is so persistently ignored and these are the people who strike fear in the minds of the megalomaniacal.

Tolerance for abuses in practice will endure for a time but only so long as the reserves of endurance exceed the demands. At which point, as in the mathematical limitations of fiat monetary policy which we will review in Volume II of the series, the environment becomes completely unsustainable and extremely unpredictable.

The American people, in particular, are now just beginning to see how truly unsustainable the abuses in political and fiscal practices have become and it would be a grave mistake for anyone to question the truth of this observation. As is often the case in unstable circumstances where the foundation of a system becomes dysfunctional, the flash-point for crisis gives absolutely no warning. It is also the perfect time for the defensive posture of the "manufactured crisis."[5]

I've given a great deal of thought to the pathogen, the cause, of this growing schism between government and the people. Is it economic? Is it social engineering? Is it monetary policy? Foreign policy? Is it fear? Has our constitutional form of government proven itself to be yet another historical failure? My answer, at least to myself, was a resounding no, it was none of these. It is far more fundamental an issue and one that is far more abstract and inconspicuous. I resolved to one general concept and it was this: The presumption of trust. In a more complete form, it may be best described in this manner:

"THE PEOPLES' GREATEST TORMENT IS NEITHER FEAR
NOR SO MUCH AS THE ABANDONMENT OF THEIR MORAL
COMPASS. NO, IT IS MORE LIKELY THAT IT IS THEIR SENSE
OF DUTY AND HONOR THAT HAS BEEN CORRUPTED BY THE

---

5   "Manufactured Crisis": The concept will be discussed more fully in Volume II: "Value Given, Value Received" of this series.

COMPLETE AND UTTER DISBELIEF THAT THEIR OWN HAVE SO
WILLINGLY AND SO RECKLESSLY VIOLATED THEIR TRUST!"[6]

A bit abstract? Try these parodies on for a bit more clarity:

*The parents of a soldier, participating in a "peacekeeping
mission" abroad, receive notice that their child suffered fatal
injuries. Explanation: Friendly Fire!*

*A spouse receives notice from an airline that her husband,
traveling to Europe for a business commitment, did not survive
the aircraft's impact with the ocean — barely 200 miles west
of the continent. Explanation: Airline cut fuel loads to save
weight.*

*A property, owned by a family for several generations, has been
confiscated by the state. Explanation: A Municipality needs to
generate more revenues and fills the requirement by promoting
mixed use development. To accomplish this, they take what you
own.*

*Individual workers loose their right to privacy and individual
right to exchange their personal industry as they see fit, without
coercion, in exchange for just compensation. Explanation:
Unions, fearing further decay in their "rolls" and revenues
acquire political influence—securing legislative coercion
through persuasive lobbyists aided by significant campaign
contributions.*

---

6   I'm referencing this particular comment of my own for quick reference for use in my closing
comment of this Volume/Series.

These are just a few examples the intent being to simply get the message in plain view: These betrayals simply should not happen. They "canst"[7] not happen. Melodramatic? I believe not!

As I move forward, consider a few fundamental beliefs that I personally aspire to and if, as it would seem, you've made it thus far along my literary journey I'm confident one will find a kinship in their common theme and upon which all might find value. I believe they are *cornerstones* of the cure and their absence in the practice of our lives and in sound governance is often the root cause of our torment:

- One must first be willing to give. It is one of the few practices worth duplicating. In its purest form, it has no expectations.

- Aim to exceed the minimum and render equality in all exchange with whomever and in whatever function you engage. I teach this principle as the *unspoken promise* and it appears this way: *Learn, as your common practice to appreciate over-delivering on the unspoken promise of what constitutes performance. When one desires to excel, one then also sets the standard for what becomes evidence of the unspoken promise! Most importantly, it also becomes your own.* This ambition becomes a critical component of what constitutes ones Character.

- Always believe there is more to do and more to do better.

- Virtue is only demonstrated and its evidence is in the mark you leave behind. We must always be certain it is one worth duplicating.

---

7   "Canst" is used here for emphasis. However, in Volume III: Valor in Prosperity, we create a unique discussion on the point more fully. I believe you will enjoy the perspective, fully!

- Faith is not held in silence, it is only ever expressed in practice.

- Character is what you do when you think no one is watching. It defines who you are.

At this point, let me share with you my observations on the malignant identifier which I refer to as the *Policy of Conflict and Selective Ideals.*

"…a sane man must appear insane in an insane society lest he be perceived as being insane…"[8]

---

8   Somewhere over the years I picked up this comment. I've expended a significant amount of time identifying its Author, I confess, with no success. Still, it seems a fabulous commentary and an appropriate statement to introduce what is to follows.

The Opening Salvo

In assembling my thoughts and observations, my goal is simply to present a progressive commentary, building as I go, on the preceding comments. All of which is to arrive at a common resolve, a refined perspective which I trust will be acknowledged by others as resonating with their own. I find that to arrive at an appropriate solution, one must first determine what is at issue. For me, frequently, I accomplish the identification phase not by first defining the fix but instead by first finding out what IS the problem and then work in reverse to find its cause. And of course, it is the "cause" that should be addressed. However in this case, this exercise is unnecessary as we can clearly see what *it* is and what *it* is, *is* toxic government! The practice, it appears to me, of government has been to adopt a process that contorts to a logic all its own.

> "GOVERNMENT HAS BECOME NOTHING MORE THAN
> THE ILLUSION OF GOVERNANCE MASQUERADING
> CONQUEST WITH THE TOOL OF CONFLICT!"

An example of this, in actual practice, is the two party (Democrat/Republican) approach. As we know the two-party concept is not a constitutional mandate; it is its own mutation and clearly not a means of perfecting the republican from of government. It is, moreover, only a means by which the purpose and outcome of government can be splintered. Having done or by doing so creates a vacuum of intention whereby the seemingly absurd becomes common practice and the distortion of government becomes, in this instance, the only thing it can ever be. This mutation occurs naturally and in a great many forms; it also, most conspicuously, has occurred right before your very eyes:

"AND THEN, SOMETHING THAT ONCE WAS, ONCE ALTERED, BECOMES SOMETHING ELSE!"

I am greatly offended when I hear members of Congress referring to a fellow congressmen as "...my esteemed colleague from across the aisle...." I find the *member-of-the-club* notion a not so subtle stab at the Ideal of *common purpose*. These types of comments are completely disingenuous particularly as they are often only a precursor to what follows which is typically adversarial in nature. In short, it simply becomes a subtle cover for its own brand of mob rule which in truth does not produce the best possible outcome and more often than not, the outcome is typically mediocre at best.

Before moving on, a few words worth reading taken from our first president's Farewell Address, September 17, 1796:

"All obstructions to the execution of the Laws, all combinations and associations, under whatever plausible character, with the real design to direct, control, counteract, or awe the regular deliberation and action of the constituted authorities, are destructive of this fundamental principle, and of fatal tendency. They serve to organize faction, to give it an artificial and extraordinary force; to put, in the place of the delegated will of the nation, the will of a party, often a small but artful and enterprising minority of the community; and, according to the alternate triumphs of different parties, to make the public

*administration the mirror of the ill-concerted and incongru-
ous projects of faction, rather than the organ of consistent and
wholesome plans digested by common counsels, and modified by
mutual interests. However combinations or associations of the
above description may now and then answer popular ends, they
are likely, in the course of time and things, to become potent
engines, by which cunning, ambitious, and unprincipled men
will be enabled to subvert the power of the people, and to usurp
for themselves the reins of government; destroying afterwards
the very engines, which have lifted them to unjust dominion."*

I can think of no better way to express the concept of Selective Ideals
than this:

"WE CAN MAKE IT MEAN WHATEVER WE WANT SO
LONG AS WE DON'T HAVE TO SAY WHAT IT IS!"

Study political rhetoric closely and you will discover that this concept
resonates in nearly every forum of government.

The idea, which I've labeled the Policy of Conflict, may be thought of
in this way:

"WE SHALL SECURE OUR PLACE BY INSURING THERE
IS NO CHALLENGE TO OUR DOING SO!"

Another way of assimilating this notion is to consider the "crab theory."
This theory suggests that a bucket full of crabs will not require being
covered to secure its content. It is said that if a single crab would
attempt an escape another will pull it down. The crustaceans, now

being in conflict with one another, are effectively neutered and pay no mind as they are whisked away to the steamer-pot!

In this way, well orchestrated as it is, the system masterfully lubricates the transmutations of sound governance in to the charade of political indifference to the same. It is, thus, not only the art form that provides the image of the dog chasing its tail, it also enables the dog to be constrained by blinders such that the animal can be made to chase any tail or no tail at all! The good news for the system is so long as the pack is busied chasing what it believes to be its tail, the system is now free to engage in inconspicuous practices (I refer to these as *Selective Ideal*) free of oversight. One might ask *why* or *how* this is possible? Well, it's really quite simple; the dogs are made busy with the illusion (these we will then identify as *Conflict*) of chasing a tail that may quite possibly be another's, may even be their own, or again, no tail at all.

So then, let us extend this imagery to view of how, in my opinion, the process has evolved to deliver the present state of national and even global affairs. There is much to say on these subjects and to keep what could easily be an exhausting essay somewhat manageable, I've settled on viewing the matter, the *Policy of Conflict* and *Selective Ideals*, through the following filters: *economic, social/entitlement and legal/ election practices*. What follows is a series of commentaries that will illustrate how, by contorting an issue to suit a preferred outcome, a conflict is enabled or created that either distracts or mutes the opposition. Whatever the outcome, there are always consequences, intended or unintended. I trust you will find the observations of value.

"WE MUST FIRST LOOK AT WHAT IS, SO THAT WE
CAN DESIGN A COURSE TO WHAT CAN BE."

Economic Implications

GLOBALISM:

RECENTLY I HAPPENED to view a PBS broadcast that included Bill Gates and his father. I'd heard much of the globalist's pitch, so none of what Mr. Gates had to say really struck me as antithetical to their view. Make no mistake, I champion the global community concept however, my concept of globalism differs dramatically from that of the globalist. With that difference in mind, my attention was drawn to one particular point made by Mr. Gates. Forgive the appearance of my *pigeon-holing* his commentary, but it is important to identify the *Selective Ideal* in this instance, particularly because it is the most common message and likewise the one most often misused to create the *Conflict* that resolves, more or less, from the globalist movement. This comment occurred during the discussion regarding access to the internet. He drew the distinction between what was suggested as an "economically viable" approach to providing universal internet access versus that which was not (economically viable). The key point to hold on to is his use of the term "economically viable" — it is *code* for the modus operandi of the globalist ideal.

It is in the subtlety of innuendo that we can often find true intention. Toward this end, here follows two very important points:

- The great danger of a monopoly is not in the nature or type of its product or service. The true danger relates to the issue of an enterprise controlling the parameters that define what becomes of *choice*. And,

- How can we proclaim that we are truly liberators if freedom is not one of the options from which one might *choose?*

The success, it could be argued, of Microsoft Corporation may be attributed less to their refining the DOS operating system[9] and moreso to the successful conquest of commanding that there was no other *choice* made available to the public. The truth of the matter is that IBM's accepting of this notion, for whatever their reason, in the development and marketing of its "PC" was to be the major turning point for what followed and, arguably, what led to Bill Gates' and Microsoft's fabulous success. To be sure, I admire the strategic aggressiveness of Microsoft and my comments are not to question their obvious financial success. However, it should never be suggested that their (Microsoft) success is a product of survival of the fittest, where fittest is defined as being the ultimate and/or supremely refined result.

To arrive at the conclusion that success is, more or less, measured by economic viability is a woefully poor argument as it is always tarnished by the realities of its intemperate conclusion. No, these are the classic non-sequiturs that if one is not alert to the subtleties of innuendo, they simply become absorbed in to the collective conscience as being a *given* and thus universally accepted as *fact*. Another example of this is "It's your patriotic duty to pay taxes…." or "…every American has the right to Universal Health Care."

---

9   The DOS Operating System was not created by Microsoft, but by Tim Paterson. Mr. Paterson worked for Seattle Computers. Micro-Soft purchased the rights to the DOS Operating System (in its infant form) in 1981 for a reported $75,000.

The great challenge or risk in presuming or asserting as a supreme thought or theory is the risk that every and any subsequent issue, idea or expression of genius that follows becomes measured, accepted or assailed based upon its conformity or "fit" with the presumed theory. The presumed risk becomes most conspicuous should the accepted theory actually be *dead wrong!* It is clear that much of what we see going wrong is the direct consequence of a dizzying array of *dead wrong* assumptions!

I think of this risk as *flat earth idolatry* and I believe this notion to be a valuable way to refine the validity of an argument or theory. It works fabulously well in evaluating economic, political and social paradigms. Let's look at a few examples:

- Consider, if you will, Christopher Columbus. In his time the general world view was that the earth was flat. It was the given paradigm of the era and the thinking of the day, largely, configured and conformed itself to this view. However, and not withstanding the world view, the earth wasn't flat at all. The critical point to get from this example is this: The world, i.e., the earth, had NEVER been flat, EVER! Yet, all that was judged or configured relative to the topographical nature of the earth was AS IF it were! I find it sort of curious to imagine what the port managers used to think when they witnessed their departing ships disappear over the horizon only to return several months later!

- Globalism finds favor as a contemporary paradigm for several reasons, however, let us address only two of the more commonly used postulates: (1.) Open border trade policies create jobs and opportunity. And, (2.) Central global governance stabilizes political and economic inequalities by eliminating political and national identity.

Each of these, once viewed through the extremely narrow lens of the globalist's perspective, in effect serves to eliminate any idea, valid or otherwise, that doesn't conform to its perspective. The *great risk!*

In other words, in the case of the United States we can clearly see what open border trade policies have done to the wealth generating economic engine of this country, not to mention the immigration, drug and security problem it has created. These are but a few blessing of globalism! In the construct of the globalist's point of view this would simply be seen as an indication of how far off the track we truly were (prior to this world vision) and proof of why globalism is the cure. Amazing how secure and stable we all would be if the world was in uniform chaos!

These notions completely ignore the fact that prior to the adoption of the world vision of globalism the economic engine of the United States, despite the parasitic overbite of government, managed to do quite well. It begs just one more step in the query: If the U.S. economic system at its peak, and well before it was strategically dissolved by the U.S. government was so proficient, then why must it be dismantled? And, if it must be dismantled and submitted to the archetype of globalism, then what theology of economic doctrine will be prescribed that will be so revolutionarily effective and different from the model it replaces? There are only two possible answers: (1) It helps to coerce the U.S. into the globalist format. Or, (2) the model is the same, albeit, an expanded and centralized version of the original.

As an aside, we might simply resolve then to the following: If it has proven to be a successful model, then why dismantle it at all? Brilliant!

It truly matter not which of the only two possible responses is chosen. Neither supports the globalist position as one can clearly see, they are in effect, one and the same: *Flat earth idolatry!*

In the case of central global governance, we can observe the same transparent simplicity of its naked flaw. What if the various global conflicts occur because folks of different countries simply prefer their own national identity? What if, they simply like it the way it is, uncluttered, unobstructed and un-imposed upon by interests that are contrary to their own? Is this not a version of what it means for one to have freedom? In the parlance of the globalist, these countries or their people might just be the very individuals that you are told need to be eliminated so that the world can be made safe for democracy. If it's their world that is being made safe for democracy, then why should they want to oppose? If it's our democracy that is being made safe, then what is it about our democracy that others should fear? Good questions? *Flat earth idolatry!*

There is no such thing as *one-size-fits-all*. Some may simply choose to wear no shoes at all! Patrick Henry, one of American History's most brilliant orators, would have understood this concept quite well.[10]

Freedom and its *expresser, liberty* have a rather unique way of accommodating this paradigm as well.

---

10   Patrick Henry (1736-1799) was among the first notable of the "Colonials" to champion the cause of exiling, forcibly, the British from the American continent. He was immortalized as one of the great champions of liberty by his speech, in 1775, "I know not what course others may take, but as for me, give me liberty or give me death."

"THERE IS A COMMON MISCONCEPTION THAT THE WORLD IS ONE AND THAT ITS PEOPLE, BEING OF A COMMON ORIGIN, ARE ONE AND THE SAME. THIS GIVES RISE TO A CONVENTIONAL BUT MISGUIDED ARGUMENT CREATING THE ILLUSION OF ONE WORLD GOVERNMENT WHERE ONE CAN FIT ALL AND ALL WILL CONFORM TO THE SAME YOKE OF IMPOSED CONFORMITY. HOWEVER, AS PLEASING AS THIS IDEA MAY SEEM, THE PREMISE IS FUNDAMENTALLY FLAWED. THE FLAW IS IN THE EXPRESSION OF THE SOUNDNESS AS IT RELATES TO THE PRINCIPLE OF FREEDOM, OF THE COMPELLING MOTIVE THAT UNDERSCORES THE PRESUMED TRUTH OF WHAT IS ASSERTED AS THE FOUNDATION FOR THE STATED AGENDA OF GLOBALISM. THE AGENDA BECOMES THEN, EITHER ONE OF ASCENSION OR ONE OF SUBMISSION! THE CONFLUENCE OF ONE WORLD GOVERNMENT IS SECURED BY FORCED SUBMISSION, WHICH CLEARLY LEAVES NO ROOM FOR THE CHOICE OF FREEDOM (THIS IS WHAT I MEAN BY ASCENSION) WHICH, OF COURSE, IS ITS PREFERRED INTENTION!

IN ITS MOST NAKED AND BARREN FORM, IT CAN ONLY BE A MANUFACTURED IDEOLOGY PERFECTED BY THE BIASED VANTAGE POINT OF 'I KNOW BETTER AND YOU KNOW NO DIFFERENCE!'"

Is it then more the case, and far more advantageous for us as a nation that what we should export are our ideals of freedom? Should it not be that we compel the global community to ascend to the ideals of freedom and the ultimate product of its perfecting by demonstrating through our own progress the potential of freedom through self-government vs. the opposing variants of tyrannical interest? Should we not hope for the global community to ascend to its potential because it is free to do so? It would seem that any option short of this is no *choice* at all but merely the only choice made available! All of which then asks the question: By whom are these choices crafted? Without a framework by which sound principles of freedom are projected, not by force, but by invitation or inspiration, and supported by demonstrated result then any ideal simply becomes the perspective *(choice)* of whoever controls or defines the intention. Agreed? In other words, if Stalin had offered the Russian people a republican from of government as an option to his own, then is it not entirely possible the Russian people might have resolved to a different course had a different course been available? We will of course, never know. However, what we do know is that here in the United States it would appear that despite the availability of freedom as a choice, why then is this choice not made available as an option? This question both troubles and fascinates me to no end!

In the pro-globalism *Policy of Conflict,* consider a few more examples of the *Selective Ideals* that are frequently used:

WE ARE ECONOMICALLY INTERCONNECTED:

Hear is the proto-typical scenario:

"THE ONLY CHOICE YOU HAVE IS THE ONE I PROVIDE YOU,"

which of course is a hopelessly biased argument. The more absurd version of this statement appears in this form:

"I HAVE TO SHOOT YOU BECAUSE THIS IS THE
ONLY GUN I OWN LOADED WITH BULLETS!"

Of course, what is conspicuous by its absence is the choice made silent: *Did you ever consider the option of simply not shooting?* One of the many conveniences of the *Selective Ideal* appears this way: the argument is crafted, the demands are defined, the choice artfully caged and the outcome known long before the speech.

The truth of the matter is this: We are economical interconnected only because the system has been maneuvered to accomplish and support this outcome. I cite, as an example, the WTO/GATT/NAFTA/CAFTA treaties that subordinated the entire federal government to a world trade body that regularly insists that our laws be modified to conform, with no public discourse and with no oversight whatsoever, to these treaties. Of the 100 senators who voted on the bill, which passed 76-24, only Senator H. Brown (R-Co) actually read the entire bill. As one would expect, he was one of only 24 who opposed it.

A French financier, James Goldsmith, testified before senate hearings on the matter. Here are a few excerpts of his comments[11]:

> *"Global free trade will force the poor of the rich countries to subsidize the rich in poor countries. What GATT means is that our national wealth, accumulated over centuries, will be transferred from a developed country like Britain to developing countries like Communist China, now building its first ocean going navy in 500 years." "China, with its 1.2 billion people, three Indochinese states with 900 million, the former Soviet republics with some 300 million, and many more can supply skilled labor for a fraction of Western costs. Five dollars*

---

11   Washington Times, December 6, 1993

in Communist China is the equivalent of a $100 wage in Europe."

U.S. Senator Ernest Hollings described the treaty in these terms:

"...the gravest mistake the U.S. has ever made on economic policy."

Knowing and understanding this, can any American really believe that the federal government operates on any principle that defers to your best interests? Is anyone really surprised that so much of the product consumed in this country is manufactured in China when the deliberate policy of the federal government was to encourage the dismantling of our nation's wealth creating engine? This country, unquestionably, is no longer capable of doing what it must to pull itself out of economic collapse. *Why?* We've no longer the means to accommodate the process, perhaps save for the high-end production processes for military procurement although this function is increasingly outsourced as well. So much for the vitality of national security as a compelling argument for sustained economic sovereignty! This nation's once dominant role, in what I refer to as the *Industry of Industry.*[12] has all but faded into the failing memory of past success.

We might also consider the following comment as the strategic ambition of globalism and as well, an appropriate irritant for inspiring true *change:*

"DARKNESS CONCEALS BOTH THE EXIT AND THE LIGHT SWITCH!"

---

12   "Industry of Industry:" Refers to the technical manufacturing resources and expertise required to produce the instruments of industry — robotics, metallurgy, casting, fiber optics, electronics etc.

When government colludes with various interests adverse to the will and interests of *The People*, we can safely conclude that there is no longer a true *free market system* remaining in the United States. However, what we do have is a *mismanaged collective-directed system*. One of the most obvious indicators of this truth is the often-used reference to "deregulation" which then should tell you all you need to know. Whether it be regulation or deregulation the simple fact that government is engaged in the process in the first place is itself sufficient proof of the substance of my statement. However, should you need further proof try these to name but a few:

- Regulations that accommodate product '"dumping."

- Regulations that allow unregulated commercial transport by foreign trucking/transport providers.

- Regulations reducing or eliminating "country of origin" labeling requirements.

- Regulations enabling the contamination of the nation's food supply.

- Regulations enabling statutory protections biased toward the pharmaceutical industry and detrimental to the public, most notably, to children.

- Deregulation of banking that institutes new regulations that void prohibitions of predatory practices and affirm the dissolution of sound monetary and fiscal practices.

These are just a few examples of government *doing* for no purpose other than to serve vested interests and not those (*The Peoples*) the system is charged to assure. I suppose you may be thinking: *Well, if the govern-*

ment doesn't do it (regulate/deregulate) then who will? If one is offended by the obvious answer to the question then feel free to do either of the following: (1) Go back to page one and start over. (2) Give your book to someone else. Or, as I would suggest, (3) Be certain to read *Volumes II: Value Given, Value Received* and *Volume III: Valor in Prosperity.*

LABOR COSTS:

What follows is yet another example of the contrived. Yes, I can produce statistical support for my comments, but to what purpose for when considering my notion of *Blind Vision*, which paraphrased implies that one really doesn't need to see evidence for what one knows to be true. Yes, the collective bargaining concept has all but destroyed the advantages of productive economic exchange in this country. Further, it might be valuable for one to ask just how does burdening the productive capacity of a nation's economic engine with the dysfunction of imbalance refines the free exchange of value? Further, as in the case with "prevailing wage" requirements, where government mandates extreme wage multipliers which systemically enforce pay scales well above and beyond practical (supportable) free-market limits, can we truly expect a beneficial yield? Regardless of the example (and many like these exist), these are all made possible by a willing and compliant government's application of *Selective Ideal* policy which molds and shapes itself to conform to the will of special interests all at the cost of self-sustaining economic independence.

Nonetheless, one has only to walk the streets of Memphis,(Tennessee), Pontiac (Michigan), Johnstown (Pennsylvania), Cincinnati (Ohio), Oakland (California) and on and on to know that the price of cheap labor is no price worth paying. How can we truly honor one another with the advocate of truth when we submit to such utter nonsense. How does a CEO of an American enterprise view the welfare of his/ her nation through the filter of *economically viable* and still assert the pretence of noble conscience?

How compelling must an argument be that supports exporting the entire lifeblood of a nation's economy to distant shores? More to the point, how valid is this argument if its premise, being cheaper labor costs, comes at the cost of an entire employment base? An *American* employment base! Further, what possible justification can there be for the depressed wage base in this country if not a direct result of these globalist views and practices? Could this be one of several reasons why immigration in the U.S. is one of an "open border policy?" That is to say, we will export our industry and import cheap labor to make a dying economy more cost effective more *economically viable*. By my own calculations, using information obtained from the Bureau of Labor and Statistics, adjusted for inflation, the average household income in this country is on par with that of 1978. This is the measure of economic viability. We've only to look at the financial health of this nation and its people to grasp the net result of these policies. I do believe we have lost our collective mind.

"WE HAVE LOST THE COMMITMENT TO THE FOUNDING
PRINCIPLES AND THE SHARED VALUE OF A REPRESENTATIVE
FORM OF GOVERNMENT. WHAT HAS MOVED IN TO REPLACE
IT IS ONLY TO ILLUSTRATE WHAT HAS BEEN LOST!"

FREE TRADE VS. PROTECTIONISM:

This is the *double-down* play otherwise known as the *two-fer Selective Ideal*. Practical wisdom has a wonderful way of surfacing at times to illustrate the error in our judgment. This occurs in many ways and in many forms. One in particular is often seen in what media outlets refer to as "gaffes." These, in my opinion, are the stress of conscience breaking through the contrived persona of the individual, typically a politician, and often at the most opportune time. One might even think of a greater tragedy being that they don't occur more often. In any case, I can think of one that occurred during the 2008 presidential campaign season that involved then presidential candidate Barack Obama. Specifically, the event that gave national prominence to "Joe the plumber" was the unscripted interchange between the candidate and this citizen. Mr. Obama's carefully crafted persona was to present him, increasingly, as the centrist candidate of choice on both social and economic issues. However, this interchange brought out a particularly powerful "gaff" which, in effect, illustrated just how far *left of left* Mr. Obama truly is, particularly in the area of "income redistribution." The comment is as follows:

> *"...And I think when you spread the wealth around,*
> *it's good for everybody,"[13]*

This is of course only one example however, it is a supremely effective one at that if for no other reason than to illustrate how politicians have little or no concept of economics and its relationship to social welfare. They see these concepts at best as interchangeable, at worst, one as a beneficial consequence of the other. In practical truth they are tied to

---

13   Source: St. Petersburg Times, 10/14/08. Transcript of recorded interchange between Mr. Obama and Joe Wurzelbacher in/at Holland, Ohio (USA).

one another however they are most definitely not consequential in the form the Political system would have you believe. The political system has lost touch with the sequence of reality as it sees government as the fuel for wealth and not, as it is, which is a direct consumer of wealth.

I know of no single successful business person whose motivation to succeed was fueled by the notion: *Gee, I'm so grateful for the government's inspiration! I can't wait to express my creative spirit brilliantly so that I might contribute more than my share to the government!* Hardly! A vibrant *wealth creating economy*[14] is the only vehicle capable of producing the means to accommodate sound, stable and self-funded social welfare programs; there is no other way.

I make this point to indicate how the distortion (*Conflict*) of an issue, in this case "free trade" (code word for *globalism*) and protectionism as practiced are, in point of fact, one and the same (the *Selective Ideal*). They are what they are regardless of the messenger. Consider the following scenario, which although a hybrid of various real world truths, is summarily applicable to many other examples:

General Motors originated as a domestic manufacturer of automobiles. The company's success in this area is well documented. As there is profit in conflict, the unions, seeking to improve their financial standing and with the aid of the elected representatives who love to court the favor of the labor force, observe the fatted calf, whose success has bred its own sort of arrogant lethargy. The company, appearing to succumb to the demands of the unions concedes; however, again, it only appears to. The company is quite influential and carries with

---

14   In Volume II of the series I discuss several economic fundamentals in the section titled *Simple Economics*. Terms such as *wealth creation, wealth consumption* and *economic engine* are more fully discussed therein. It is an integral part of the whole discussion one in which the reader will surely want to engage.

it significant economic clout. Addressing the issue of increased labor costs and finding it beneficial toward its desire to avoid the increasing tax burden, GM moves to create alternative manufacturing facilities offshore. It accomplishes this in many ways including but not however limited to acquiring interests (partial or complete) of existing operations on foreign soil or simply by constructing their own. This has several beneficial results, among them being: (1.) broader market penetration for their brand; (2.) outside sourcing for domestic (final) assembly; (3.) beneficial tax treatment from "transfer pricing"[15] manipulation; and (4.) greater control of labor costs (more labor intensive processes are performed in cheaper labor markets).

We have, in this illustration, three dominant players: the union, the company, and the government, each with its own Selective Ideal which is promoted through the Policy of Conflict. All of which, it should be added, have contorted the ideal of the self-government model beyond its purpose and its intention.

Here's where it gets even more entertaining. Let me present an interesting question. If you are a party to the globalist idea and/or agenda, whether as a politician, a financier or a corporate enterprise, how can you lose by claiming ownership of both sides of the argument particularly in the instance where your interests are served at both ends? Yes, you're correct, there is no apparent loss.

The politicians can claim they are legislating to preserve domestic General Motors by giving it favorable financial backing, or government

---

15   Transfer Pricing: The cost assigned to a product or component between/among common interests within a domestic environment as well as outside (foreign) this environment. Often, the practice is to increase the "transfer price" of a product or component to favorable advantage the taxable event. The appearance, domestically, of a higher product cost reduces the illustrated taxable income of a product.

military contracts, which keeps "hard working Americans employed" (a curious form of *protectionism*). The corporate enterprise is also rewarded as it is able to continue to bring product in to the country (so called "free trade") with the aid of the government and as we can see, the politicians will do just about anything to preserve their influence even and most audaciously when this influence is at the cost of your own. And lastly, the financier is delighted either way since wherever the process, he has strategically positioned political influence, he is well resourced and available to meet the financial demands no matter the location. There is profit in conflict!

"WHAT IS LEFT ARE SPOILS THAT NONE OF THE PARTICIPANTS
CAN USE. THEY ARE NO LONGER ECONOMICALLY VIABLE
AS YOU HAVE NO INHERENT BENEFIT REMAINING!"

When considering the mantra of a globalist, it is easy to see that there is no such thing as viable "free trade" and no such ambition as true "protectionism." I believe, as we will discuss in both Volumes II and III more fully, that in fact, a nation thrives best when both "free trade" and "protectionism" are fully functioning principles. The use of these terms in contemporary politics and in media references, however, are used only as an art form bearing no real substance and only used to achieve a desired outcome. The purpose is to spread the illusion that "the people" are the beneficiaries of this *new world order* whose true intention is economic and social welfare. It is true that if we depress the standards of the people of this or any country, *then we surely do become the equal of all* by being just another cog in the global family of third world nations!

In reality, these processes of *free trade* and *protectionism* exist simultaneously and in practice are sustainable and best explained as follows:

"FREE TRADE IS A NECESSITY FOR ECONOMIC HEALTH AS
IT EXPANDS THE BOUNDARY OF MARKETS, THE FREE AND
UNINTERRUPTED EXCHANGE OF IDEAS AND ENABLES THE NOBLE
PERFECTION OF MANS' RELATIONSHIPS. HOWEVER, WITH
NO PROTECTION OF A NATION'S NOBLE COURSE, ITS VIRTUE,
ITS SECURITY AND ITS INDUSTRY, THERE CAN BE NO SUCH
NOTION OF FREE TRADE, THERE IS ONLY ITS CONQUEST!"

OUR NATIONAL/ECONOMIC INTERESTS AND SAFE FOR DEMOCRACY:[16]

Another *two-fer* and yet another illustration of the contorting of a concept to suit an objective. We often hear a president or congressmen posturing on an issue armed with either (and often both) of these statements proselytizing the matter at hand as being in "our national interests" or that some action in which this nation is engaged is making the world "safe for democracy."

I have become increasingly suspicious of these kinds of declarations largely because of how frequently they have been used over the last 50 years and how little economic reward or security gains they've produced for the people of this country. If something is truly in the interest of our nation, and when I speak of *nation* I always mean *The People*, then should not these *interests* at some point be paying dividends to the

---

16 "National" or "economic" interests references are, as in this case, used interchangeably. Just know that I will alternate the use of these however, unless specified, their meaning is uniform.

American people as compensation for their sacrifice? Surely no politician could look at a citizen and point out the stunning successes of our legislative practices, immigration policy, education system, social fiber, national security, economic and financial stability and suggest, with any degree of honesty, *Look at how far we've come!* Yet another compelling force behind why I see no reason for *The People* to continue bearing so thankless and unproductive a burden.

Pretense (which the anointed refer to as *economic interests*) seems to warrant the deployment of our nation's most cherished resource, our uniformed men and women. For their lives we gain sorrow and the permanent stain upon our souls and for this, we gaze in to nothingness. Is this why we consign our own stores of true wealth, to enrich those who would pull upon the strings of yet another armed marionette as an extension of their *economic interests* and *personal gain*? This, it would seem, has become the stage and face of war which has become known by many names.

"WHEN THE FINAL BREATH HAS BEEN EXPRESSED AND SHOULD THERE BE BUT ONE TO REMOVE THE VEIL, WE WILL THEN KNOW WE HAVE SACRIFICED SO MUCH FOR ABSOLUTELY NOTHING AT ALL!"

Never doubt for a moment that I, along with millions of others, would stand to defend the honor of this nation, our people and our constitutional values however, should our actions not first be shaped by and thus be an extension of these same *values?* I believe so, as,

"IT IS OFTEN THE SUBTLE HAND OF VIRTUE THAT BEGETS THE CONVERT ONCE AN ENEMY!"

If the economic interests are justly those of this or any nation then by all means said nation has the right, the duty, to secure them. If this or any nation's sovereign boundaries find themselves advanced upon by a migrant horde then by all means, they should be summarily repelled with great prejudice. Barring this, I believe it to be in this nation's interests only to protect its people and its economic interests through the superiority of our ideals and our practices. Should any threat occur to our land or our people, it should be dispatched by the superior capabilities of our military.

"NEVER GIVE A TYRANT AN AUDIENCE. THE SILENT
RESOLVE OF SOUND JUDGMENT WILL YIELD THE SUCCESS
YOU DESIRE AND IN THIS, BE YOUR BEST ADVOCATE!"

With these thoughts on globalism in mind, I am left with this question and final thought on this particular subject: What is wrong with our judgment and our practices that as an extension of this country, or should I say in the name of its people, we should have to make the world safe for our brand of democracy? I should think a good question upon which all should direct their attention.

"Observe good faith and justice towards all Nations; cultivate peace and harmony with all. Religion and Morality enjoin this conduct; and can it be, that good policy does not equally enjoin it? It will be worthy of a free, enlightened, and, at no distant period, a great Nation, to give to mankind the magnanimous and too novel example of a people always guided by an exalted justice and benevolence. Who can doubt, that, in the course of

time and things, the fruits of such a plan would richly repay any temporary advantages, which might be lost by a steady adherence to it? Hence, likewise, they will avoid the necessity of those overgrown military establishments, which, under any form of government, are inauspicious to liberty, and which are to be regarded as particularly hostile to Republican Liberty."[17]

---

17   George Washington: Farewell Address, September 17, 1796. It should be noted that the last sentence does not appear in the Presidents address in the form as presented. In its actual placement, however, the context is identical. The entire text of President Washington's "Farewell Address" appears in Appendix II of this manuscript. I encourage all to read and treasure his counsel.

Social/Entitlement Implications

"The democracy will cease to exist when you take away from those who are willing to work and give to those who would not."

"It is incumbent on every generation to pay its own debts as it goes. A principle which if acted on would save one-half the wars of the world."

"I predict future happiness for Americans if they can prevent the government from wasting the labors of the people under the pretense of taking care of them."[18]

I NEVER INTENDED this to be an historical retrospective on Thomas Jefferson; however, nearly 200 years later, one most assuredly will appreciate their contemporary significance. They define the perfect ideal of government, the absence of which, as we will explore in the commentary that follows, effectively reveals the *Selective Ideal.* The *Conflict*, as well, is equally conspicuous as the product of government's efficient use of *social splintering* whereby mob rule becomes the means by which the process is exalted.

---

18   All three of these comments belong to Thomas Jefferson.

I maintain that success in all our noble pursuits, be it economic, social or justice is directly related to the degree we preserve individual liberty by forcing the government to avoid interference in these lofty pursuits. Observing the present state of the republic the objective conclusion must be that government has served masterfully in the capacity of a biased obstructionist. What follows, in no particular order, are a few examples of *targets of opportunity* illustrating the government's defiance of constitutional mandates and prohibitions:

TAXATION:

Equality among our people is an ideal which has yet to be resolved. This is yet another illustration of what is meant by the comment "… the unknown good intrusive government silences." For all Americans, this should be deeply troubling particularly as it so fundamental a constitutional principle. Equality has no variants; it is either a systemic mandate that becomes a by-product of sound governance and culture or it is not. There is no more or less equal as it relates to the fundamental right of self-determination embodied by, "We hold these truths to be self-evident that all men are created equal…." There is no more or less.

I've often asked why this is this case. The only answer I can muster is this: *Inequality pays and it pays well.* It pays on the issue of race because truck-loads of money cam be made in perpetuating disintegration. It pays in the issue of religion (moral issues) because there are perceived opportunities by defying a moral and just social structure. It pays in the black hole of entitlements for the obvious reason that *he who has been entitled, is entitled to be paid!* And lastly, it works effectively in the *Conflict* of politics by creating a forum for the politician.

However, it is in the supreme dysfunction of taxation that the purest form of inequality persists most efficiently as it fits nicely in the model of the most vulgar of all projected inequalities. It is the means by which the ultimate form of injustice is bred: *Economic class warfare.* This form of warfare has long been an effective management tool of the collectivist. It serves as both an efficient means to control a people and to engage their fears.

The divisive arguments are never ending; here are but a few:

- The poor pay a disproportionate share of their income.

- The rich can afford to pay more in taxes.

- There is a need to control generational wealth accumulation.

- Taxation is a required revenue source for funding government spending.

- The government requires a population "data mining" source.

- There exists a need, by way of a structured mechanism, for preserving income redistribution for social engineering policies and practices.

- Tax and/or revenue enforcement actions are an effective tool for government intervention into the private sector.

And my favorite,

- It's your patriotic duty to pay taxes. A most idiotic notion and integral to the social-engineering metaphor.

Well, suffice it to say, these contorted notions are preferred only by those who seek an advantage. I summarily dismiss them as predatory and not relevant to a *just* system of taxation.

"ON CONSTITUTIONAL GROUNDS ALONE, I'LL SUGGEST TO YOU THAT AS A FUNCTION OF A POLITICIAN'S COMMITMENT TO THEIR PATRIOTIC DUTY, THEY MIGHT CONSIDER INSURING THAT AS LITTLE TAX IS DRAWN FROM THE PEOPLE AS POSSIBLE, NOT MORE!"

To arrest the wealth of any person purely on the grounds of his ability to produce defies all foundations of reason. To tax the incentive of an individual is to penalize his/her having the inspiration to pursue any lawful means of prosperity! Further, to configure an argument supporting this practice of conscripting productivity to somehow appear noble or just is the quintessential manifestation of the *Selective Ideal!*

Yes, a tax system is necessary even though, as with most Americans, I fail to see a connection with the ideal of patriotism or as an extension of *duty*. Which, by the way, begs the questions: Duty to whom? And, in a republican form of democracy, should we not apply the concept of *duty* uniformly or is the ideal only the burden of a select few and thereby only equally beneficial to only those who have no such *duty?* While it is appropriate for there to be some form of revenue generating mechanism, it should not be one of a perpetual nature assessed against the productive means of the individual. Doing so places the government first in line and the individual at the end. How is this equality, how is that just and how is this emblematic of freedom?

The tax code is a maniacal maize of counter productive and biased regulations and effectively institutionalizes piracy. It is beneficial to none but those who can coerce beneficial effect through influencing a congressman or by those who control the gavel of the World Trade Organization (WTO)[19]. It should come as no surprise that in an era of record breaking corporate revenues actual tax receipts, as a percentage of total corporate revenue, have consistently moved downward[20]. Conversely, the individual tax burden, as a percentage of income, has gone steadily in the opposite direction.

Under the current system, for every dollar earned, an individual is taxed no less than 10 times on the same dollar! You earn it, you're taxed – six times[21], you save it, you're taxed, you invest it, you're taxed, you spend it, you're taxed and when you die, should you have anything left, your heirs stand to lose upwards of 50% of what otherwise should have been your legacy.

"I PREDICT THAT THE NEXT GREAT CONSCRIPTION OF YOUR WEALTH GENERATING CAPABILITIES WILL SOON MAKE ITS APPEARANCE IN THE UNITED STATES. IT IS ONE OF THE MOST CONSPICUOUS ACTS OF A DYING ECONOMIC PARADIGM AND WITHOUT A DOUBT THE WORST POSSIBLE FORM OF ENIGMATIC REVENUE GENERATING YET DEVISED: THE VALUE ADDED TAX (VAT). WHEN ANY GOVERNMENT HAS BECOME ACCUSTOMED TO UNCHECKED POLICY AND FISCAL PRACTICES EXPERIENCES THE VISE OF EXCESS, ITS ONLY CHOICE

---

19   Pursuant to the U.S. participation in the WTO, any U.S. law that violates these Treaty provisions, either as written or as adjudicated by the WTO, must be modified to a compliant result.

20   Source: U.S. Office of Management and Budget. Budget of the United States Government, Historical Tables, Fiscal Year 2009. Compared with Internal Revenue "Business Tax Statistics" as of 2006.

21   Payrol Taxes: Fed & State Income Tax, Social Security, Medicaid, Medicare, State Disability.

IS TO FURTHER TIGHTEN ITS OWN PREDATORY GRIP. LIKE ANY ADDICT, IT HAS NO OTHER CHOICE BUT FURTHER ACTS OF PIRACY!"

With any progressive tax system, in effect, one's earnings have a progressively diminishing yield. Is it any wonder that what we perceive as only the outgoing tide is only a precursor to an economic tsunami! Let me offer you a slight variation on an old anecdote:

"YOU COME INTO THIS WORLD WITH NOTHING AND
YOU LEAVE WITH NOTHING AND THE GOVERNMENT
WANTS TO BE SURE THIS CYCLE PERSISTS!"

I recommend being sure to visit the discussion of *Simple Economics* in Volume II of this series for a thorough review of the consequences of a draconian tax system. The only thing more damaging than the current tax system is the fact that not one President or Congress has been willing to address it. Proof, in my opinion, that government prefers the *Conflict* over resolution. It does so because it pays so nicely!

SOCIAL/ENTITLEMENT PROGRAMS:

As in the case of taxation, it is the government who becomes the adversary in the creative *Conflict*. In the area of social spending, the government perfects a force multiplier by adding our own countrymen in to the mix. Not only is this economically counterproductive, the presumed notion of entitlement and the manner in which it is used has itself evolved into a process that has universally contaminated the culture of this country. It has penetrated the fabric of the nation to such a degree that *Webster's Dictionary* has a specific definition for the word entitlement:"A government program providing benefits to members of a specified group." How can a representative form of government take the product of a people's industry and give it to a "specified group" and call this equality? How can this be justified? How can this be anything but what it is? *Thievery!* One might just as well go in to another person's home and on the grounds of entitlement, take their personal property with the justification being that you have none of your own.

To capture the attention and patronage of *The People* the government offers promises that it knows it simply cannot keep. More *flat earth idolatry!* People are entrapped and ultimately enslaved by the false belief that government can and should make these (entitlement) programs available. In short, this expectation promotes social disintegration by defining and legislating the taking from the so called *haves* and giving to the *have nots.*

> "IT IS IMPORTANT TO NOTE THAT WHAT THE
> GOVERNMENT APPEARS ABLE TO GIVE IT ACQUIRES
> FIRST BY TAKING. IT OCCURS NO OTHER WAY!"

Further, it enables the government to engage in what amounts to a protected enterprise unburdened by a systemic requirement of most *for profit* concerns — that of a tangible and a positively measured result. If the government fails to keep a promise, it simply entitles itself to expand the framework of the formerly failed promise. Combine this motive with an ever increasing public consciousness that has adapted to the *Selective Ideal* known as the *political industry of entitlement,* and the politician has a mandate to expand and make permanent this unique industry's place in the political hierarchy of the process!

Perhaps you doubt this statement. Consider the modest beginnings of Social Security and its progressive expansion to the unfunded behemoth it is today.[22] The concept, which was rooted in the idea of providing a "social safety net" has morphed in to a full blown life-support system. And, as is the case with all parasitic species, its only means of sustenance occurs from the perpetual feeding upon its host.

It is interesting to note the history of Social Security's origins. President Roosevelt, ever the consummate collectivist and master manipulator, responded to a series of New Deal defeats at the hands of the once functional Supreme Court. He did so by threatening congress with a bill that in effect would enable him to "stack" the court by expanding the number of justices. The six-month long battle was resolved by ceding in favor of the president's wishes. Nothing like a *crisis* to pave the way for accommodation by subversive collation, otherwise known as *The Policy of Conflict and Selective Ideals!*

As if the disaster and cumulative maize of these life-support systems isn't sufficient to suffocate your ambitions, get ready, we've a new one being programmed into the *ideals* of the nation. Yes, *Universal Health Care*. A concept that has proven absolutely anemic in its ability to provide effective service to the sick and has proven to be financially unsustainable in every country the concept has been deployed. Yet,

"IT SEEMS THAT THE DANCE OF ECONOMIC AND SOCIAL DEATH WILL NOT BE COMPLETE WITHOUT THE GOVERNMENT PROVING ITSELF WORTHY OF CREATING YET ANOTHER FORM OF FAILURE!"

---

22   The current debt (federal) @ 4/9/09, per the U.S. Treasury is $11 trillion estimated to increase by $2 trillion in the current fiscal year alone, and, this is only the public debt and does not include private debt nor the unfunded estimated $100 trillion unfunded Medicaid Medicare and Social Security demands. It is estimated these alone add $1 trillion per year to the aggregate unfunded amount. This number does not include the annual "debt service costs."

As is the case with many of the topics we discuss in this introductory volume, further commentary and topical resolutions are required. Rest assured that I have compiled a variety of thoughtful resolutions and, as in the case of national/universal health care, I address each in the final volume of this series *Volume III: Valor in Prosperity.*

The ONLY thing the government does with absolute perfection and efficiency is waste money, conscript value, debase individual rights and perpetuate its ability to do the same. I challenge any individual to name one successful government program, deferential to Constitutional ideals, that delivers on its promise. Can you name one that is economically self-sustaining?

> *"To take from one because it is thought that his own industry and that of his father's has acquired too much, in order to spare to others, who, or whose fathers have not exercised equal industry and skill, is to violate arbitrarily the first principle of association—'the guarantee to every one of a free exercise of his industry and the fruits acquired by it"* [23]

I truly do believe we have a duty as individuals, not as a government,[24] to provide appropriate care for the elderly and the infirm who do not possess the resources of family or finance. But to place the financial burden of funding an entire *whole life support system* on the back of the people is both a breach of republican principles and financially and economically unsustainable. More over, it's just plain WRONG!

Why is it financially and economically unsustainable? Well, it would be unfair for me to not address, at least preliminarily, the question here

---

23   Thomas Jefferson: Note in Destutt de Tracy's "Political Economy," 1816.

24   The mandate should only ever be one from *The People* and never from the government.

so let me tease the discussion with concepts I introduce in the next volume. Consider if you will, that the notion is unsustainable, as are all government entitlement programs, for several reasons of which the following are just a few:

- Government programs exist/occur only as the result of *conscription*. That is the ability of government, either by fiat, legislative or administrative action, to assign legitimacy to its action simply by the act of doing it.

- When government *conscripts* value/wealth by or through this method it defeats the mechanism that creates the wealth it "conscripts."

- As *conscripted wealth*, now having been removed from the national economic engine, it is no longer reliable *seed-stock* for further *wealth creating* enterprise. However, having done so allows Industry to discover (by necessity) that it can also feed on the conscripted wealth by acquiring control or interest in the political process. In effect what one ends up with, as we see in (largely) both federal and state government, is a self-propagating economic enterprise of entitlement programs on which Industry[25] (both public and private sectors) practice the parasitic art of sustainability. There are few industries in the U.S. and/or their global counterparts who do not feed, in one form or another, off the U.S. economy or taxpayer.

- The consequence of these, and there are many, is a complete disintegration of an economic system which then survives only by and on a government's ability to spend. It is

---

25   The use of the term "industry" is intended in the broadest terms. In this application, it can mean industrial, manufacturing, defense, technology and services as well.

important to note that government spending is the largest component of U.S. GDP and this is why, primarily, the U.S. is a dying (if not already dead) economic engine.

In its simplest and most uncluttered form the notion of unsustainability, whether in literal or figurative form, resides on the issue of resource. The government operates on or in a financial paradigm that revolves around *conscription* and *debt generation* methodologies as a means to generate revenue. In short, the government sustains its spending habits by taking wealth through various means, the most conspicuous being direct income tax, and the most inconspicuous being what I refer to as *social enrichment* aggregators such as cigarette taxes, various excise and *use* penalty fees such as *gas guzzler taxes*. There is a veritable plethora of these (types of) revenue generating mechanisms. What the government isn't able to accumulate in this manner it simply borrows, i.e., *debt generation.*

The problem with this approach resolves again to the issue of *resource* and the concept of whether *resource* occurs first or prior to wealth being created or if *resource* is a product of wealth creation. Not only does the government appear to believe, evidenced by its actions, that *resource* occurs before *wealth is created* it also believes that it is the arbiter of the *wealth creation* function. I will discuss this issue and present a few interesting examples later in this series but for now I, like many, agree with the parabolic notion that

> "YOU CAN'T SPEND WHAT YOU DON'T HAVE AND
> YOU DON'T HAVE WHAT YOU DON'T EARN!"

By redirecting wealth, or we might also say, by the act of *conscripting wealth*, this governmental actions alter the kinetic force that lies back of the engine that creates wealth which, I stress, should always be understood as the *first* order of business. None the less, by doing so, it vaporizes the mechanisms (the economic engine) resource generating facility that would, if left to perfect its ability, *self-fund* what the political engine has adopted as it's self-directed economic enterprise of entitlement programs.

I must, for now, conclude the discussion and move on, however, before doing so, there is one final point that is a particularly disturbing component the likes of which has been ignored entirely. It is the component of the science of economics that is largely unobserved and misunderstood. I think of it as *physiological/sociological-economics, (a.k.a., physio/socio-economics).* I use this term to identify the following: *The practices and tendencies of how economic actions/events or enterprises orient themselves intuitively addressing or responding to sociological/ political preferences or issues.* As in the case of water, it can both quench your thirst or one can drown in it. Regardless of one's intention, know this; the outcome will be predictable and certain. Fortunately, with all things of consequence, the cause is always identifiable.

RELIGION:

There is an increasing attack on religion in this country having, at its core, the bent argument of *separation of church and state.* Suffice it to say the distortions, in their most typical form, have pushed the foundational reliability of the argument to an all time low. The assault is growing and I place the blame for this smartly upon all three branches of government and to a lesser degree, faith-based organizations as well.

Whether you are a devout practitioner of faith or not, any person of conscious, by observing general practices throughout our culture can testify to an accelerating departure from moral and/or civil decorum. One can observe examples of this departure from the absence of simple courtesies to our demonstrated indifference to the most sacred of all, the value of human life. It is not so much that reckless behavior is more prevalent, it is rather the increasing unwillingness to recognize and identify it for what it is. The following comment defines, simultaneously, the obstacle that is both the manifestation of the *Selective Ideal* and the *Conflict.*

"CONTEMPT IS OFTEN ONLY THE GREAT FEAR OF CONSCIENCE
WHOSE IMAGE IS STARING AT YOU IN DISGUST!"

Freedom is not perfected by simply finding means with which one might indulge one's impulses. Freedom is in the virtue of comprehending the distinction between *Though I can, I ought not!* An alternative approach to the thought is to present it in this way;

"FREEDOM IS EXPRESSED FREELY WITH THE UNDERSTANDING AND
SELF-RESTRAINT THAT YOU MAY NOT BE AT LIBERTY TO DO SO!"

If a people are to benefit from a cohesive social structure they must ultimately resolve to share its bias which of course then becomes consistent with and emblematic of their shared resolve. Do we all not maintain the *shared resolve* of the *cohesive social structure* that has at its core "We hold these truths to be self-evident...?" Is this not an adhesive bond, is this not a valid basis for a code of conduct that a man or woman of conscience may find a common and unifying belief? I pose these as questions deliberately with the hope that one will rest on the idea for a time meditating on an individual's own compass and come to a thoughtful resolution. I truly believe it will be *common* to all. This is of course, my hope!

As the Declaration of Independence "…unanimous declaration…" refines and the Constitution expresses by reference to "We the People.…", an assembly of said People must also promote and preserve this ideal. It is the core ideal that is so precisely and fabulously pronounced in both opening salvos of each of these documents. Indeed, this shared resolve is a *species of religion* by itself.

It matters not whether one is a Christian, a Jew, a Hindu, a Buddhist, a Muslim or for that matter, agnostic, to benefit from this structure. Indeed, history has shown that the republican form of government is inclusive rather than exclusive *particularly* as it deals with religion. I believe that this is precisely the distinction of "separation of church and state." In other words, one is free to participate in the benefits of a structure without being forced to profess a specific preference to a selected religious dogma. This however, does not imply that there is *no ideal.* In fact, the fundamental agreement perfecting the structure is that the individual is free to define for themselves what *it* is even if *it* means, for them, nothing at all. Which then, I might add, becomes that individual's *God* from which or by whom this person is *endowed.* What the concept of "separation of church and state" most definitely does not entitle is the forced abandonment of conscience. As a Nation and as a People, we are and will pay an ever increasing price for our indifference! Whatever your *Creator* may be, again, even if, which I must confess defies all forms of reason that I know of, your *Creator* is no *thing* at all, it is not nor has it ever been the domain of Government or the Judiciary to determine or otherwise purloin and enforce its own rendition. It is however, the specific intent of the Constitution that one's personal design and practice not be interfered with.

The truth of the matter is, yes, I am a *Roman Catholic* and though I hold more to a monotheist's system of belief than I do to the pure form of Catholicism I admit this is largely semantics[26]. Nonetheless, I struggle to find the reason for proselytizing the *Conflict* on the issue of religion unless it is the possibility that there is something to gain by planting the seed as a course toward social anarchy. Yes, the founding documents of this country effervesce with the tone of Judeo Christianity, suggesting that we can "separate" the fundamentals concomitant with this reality is yet another example of both a puerile and feeble minded prevarication[27]. The simple fact is that the republican form of government came in to existence, persisted and succeeded to the degree that it has because it is an extension of these principles; its lineage is in harmony with the canons of Judaism, Mosaic and Natural Law. So let us once and for all put the issue to rest and universally resolve that as a basis for sound governance, it works! As a construct or code of conduct, who among us can honestly say that there can be any successful or peaceable social order without a forum from which to define what is acceptable and what is not? Without this construct, then what are the defining filters for that which is enduring and that which is prohibited?

I recall a comment which I must confess my inability to locate the source (and to whomever it may be I extend appropriate credit), nonetheless, it is worth repeating here: "Are the principles espoused in the

---

26   There is much more to this statement so a word caution for one who might find this statement troubling; might I suggest you find consolation in the last six words of the referenced sentence. "…I admit this is largely semantics."

27   There have been several polls over the years that suggest a staggering 92% of Americans believe in "God" or a "Devine Presence". There are others (polls) still, who suggest 76% say they are "Christian".

Bible sound because they are in this book or are they in the Bible simply because they are sound?" Acknowledging as I do a personal bias, I'll leave the ultimate outcome of this observation to you, the reader.

However one resolves the previous comment, I observe that the principles that lie behind Judeo-Christianity are as old as light. They existed long before man made his first footprint and they will exist long after his last. What matters the messenger if the message provides the template of a replicable and pure ideal that yields a magnificent and sustainable result.

"IF THE MESSAGE THAT LIES BEHIND THE TEN COMMANDMENTS WERE TO HAVE APPEARED AS A HOLOGRAM ON THE WINDSHIELD OF A HONDA CIVIC HYBRID OR ON THE WALL OF A METH-LAB WOULD IT MAKE IT EASIER TO ACCEPT? OR IS IT THAT WE HAVE BECOME SO WEAK-MINDED THAT WE EXCISE CHERISHING AND EXTOLLING SOUND PRINCIPLES FOR FEAR OF BEING ANONYMOUS!"

For anyone to champion, particularly to a child, the notion that there is *no good in goodness* and that a productive, peaceful and benevolent social structure can be advocated absent that very foundation that defines its structure is nothing short of self-indulgent and sociopathic.

My final comments on the subject relate to its function within a social structure and its consequent public emissaries:

As human beings our lives and interactions with one another are a seemingly unending string of conscious thoughts and decisions. Every decision we make has at its root a series of choices that conclude, prior to action (mental or physical), as a *go* or *no go* choice. The mere fact that you make a choice is an expression of bias in one form or another.

The process that expresses this bias is based on whatever presumed filters (ideals and/or compass, sense of right/wrong) one uses to discern between all possible choices. This process occurs in fractions of split seconds, so it may appear as a subconscious thought, but it only appears that way based largely on the degree with which our belief system has matured in to a pattern. Only when faced with a (new) personal preference that conflicts with the belief system does the process slow down to appear to be conscious, i.e., a deliberate, specific and calculated process which, to conform to your personal preference, is often situational and therefore requires a sort of remanufactured belief system to accommodate/justify your desired preference (otherwise known as "situational ethics").

Take for example the issue of abortion: As a man I confess my personal belief system is on auto-pilot as I see the issue clearly as one surrounding the sanctity of life whose very existence revolves around the womb of the child's mother. The sanctity of life ideal that I hold states that a fetus is *a life* and as I am not able to separate the fundamental truth of the human reproductive function as being anything other than to perpetuate human life. I can find no reason to support the concept that abortion is anything other than what it is, which is the taking of a life.

Now, enter the opposing view and consider how the process slows down and appears to become a conscious process. In stating the preceding I am presuming that the *sanctity of life ideal* is generally and universally accepted by all, women and men. Any individual whose views are different from my own (which by the way is your right and one I wholly support) must still, ultimately, wrestle with the very same issue. In other words, as to the *sanctity of life ideal*, the individual will, regardless, have to choose one or the other, it is unavoidable. One might suggest that what appears in the public discourse as *choice* is precisely that (*choice*); however, I believe that in truth it is actually more an issue of choosing between accepting a burden or responsibility or choosing to dispense with said burden or responsibility by aligning with others of similar view who enable, by co-endorsement, the desired point of view. Whatever one's position is, no matter how or in what way one resolves to an ultimate decision, the mechanism, one's belief system, is what is used to arbitrate one's ultimate choice. The caliber of your character is the measure or extent to which you apply it with consistency no matter the difficulty. I would suggest that any process short of this is the very point where *impulse driven* actions begin.

The point of this illustration is to demonstrate why and how a belief system is inseparable from our existence as individuals and how as individuals we apply these beliefs in a social structure. From a social engineering perspective, I believe it adequately illustrates how the processes arbitrated by judicial and/or government actions seeks to detach the individual from his or her belief system. We might even find that the power of government is used, deliberately, for this purpose. That is, to separate the individual from one's individual belief system to one that is prescribed by government[28]. Certainly, I believe it safe to say this approach makes it quite easy to control the masses! Does it not? By the way, if one doubts this observation consider that this may be the very reason citizenry sit idly by when the ovens are turned on or when a neighbor's family member is abducted and/or sold into slavery. I often wonder how the advocate of "choice" might change his/her mind if it were their life whose future was being arbitrated!

---

28   It might be interesting for one to now consider, in this comment, what is meant by "Separation of Church and State"!

It is my conviction that the measured degree of what defines a noble and just culture is the extent to which said culture's common beliefs compel and extol practices that are consistent with its fundamentals, e.g., "Life, Liberty and the Pursuit of Happiness" no matter how extreme the efforts to assert the contrary. On this very point, I believe we might sit in judgment of ourselves for quite some time.

It is for these reasons, among others, that the moment we introduce or witness issues of social engineering through the use of judicial and/or legislative force we simultaneously run into the consequential practices of *Selective Ideals* and the *Policy of Conflict*. It is also why it is ever more important that when these issues occur a compass of ideals, a code of conscience, be ever present. Believing that it is possible to accomplish, blindly, sound governance without the vision/aid of a belief system is to attempt an escape from reality. To expect that in the public domain of governance, particularly on issues revolving around *choice,* that contentious issues will not become filtered through the mechanism of personal bias is to assert an unsupportable conclusion. To that end, consider what follows as what I have come to believe is yet another *fundamental truth*.

"WHAT YOU THINK, BECOMES WHAT YOU KNOW AND WHAT
YOU KNOW CONTROLS WHAT YOU DO! INEVITABLY!"

It is after all, inescapable human condition! Once an individual breaches a socially contracted prohibition, its effects penetrate both the Individuals and the Social conscience and there's simply no reversing its imprint. No? Who ever would have thought that one would have to explain to a child the actions of a U.S. President that included the topical content of "oral sex?" Try taking that one back!

The actions of an individual matter immensely, particularly those which the system will tell you are "private" and not relevant to public conscience or discourse. However, as we all know, they are intensely relevant, more directly, they are the very actions that matter most precisely because they occur when no one is watching and the tension of public scrutiny is completely absent. For goodness sake, does anyone really think that Richard Nixon's actions would have been socially acceptable so long as no one knew the Watergate break-in had occurred? We might simply just accept one of many unchangeable laws of nature:

"THE SOCIAL FABRIC OF OUR NATION RECORDS THE MEMORY OF OUR ACTIONS. THERE ARE MANY IN BRILLIANT COLOR; THOUGH AMIDST A FIELD OF OUR REMARKABLE THERE LIES THE SHADE OF PENITENT REGRET."

Legal/Election Implications

"TO BELIEVE THAT IN ANY HUMAN INTERACTION ONE CAN
SUPPRESS THE PERSONAL BIAS OF ONE'S MORAL COMPASS
- AS IF IT WERE ONLY A TEMPTATION OF NATURE - AND
SIMULTANEOUSLY HOLD TO AN ANTITHETICAL POINT CONTRARY
TO SAID MORAL COMPASS IS TO SUGGEST THAT ONE CAN STAY
DRY IN A STORM BY STEPPING BETWEEN DROPS OF RAIN."

THE TRUTH OF and the impossibility of this belief is regularly demonstrated through the bias of the judicial and legislative process. How can one suggest that a person's personal/moral views do not migrate in to the judicial/legislative process? If that weren't the case, then explain/justify *Roe v. Wade*. Explain/justify the opinions surrounding the removal of prayer from public school? The proof of this observation occurs by reversing the claim. Observe how these decisions (being the *Selective Ideal*), as either a judicial or legislative mandate, become representative only of the select few and not representative of *The People's* will. (This might be an appropriate time to review the content of footnote #27.)

Have you, like me, ever wondered who represents your interests before the Supreme Court? I know I have. Who represents the will of the people in matters where the courts, in various contests, demonstrate indifference to the Constitution? This question may seem patently juvenile but consider the question from the point of view not of judicial preference or spontaneous maniacal trend or impulse, but truly from the perspective of a representative form of government particularly when the will of the majority has spoken. I have no answer simply because there is apparently, none. It would seem that the attorney general might play an active role but typically, as they are political appointments, there is no continuity of interest in preserving the constitutional rule of law. True, the Supreme Court itself was intended to take up the mantle of constitutional preservation; however the Court has largely and effectively been cornered by congressional and presidential derelictions. I believe, if only to this comment alone, this to be the single greatest and most lasting failure of the Supreme Court.

No, unfortunately the will of the people and constitutional rule of law is left to, of all possible organizations, the *American Civil Liberties Union (ACLU)*, the self-anointed protector of the people. However, I must ask, how is this possible? How can a third party of this type have "standing" before the highest court of the Land without, at the least, any legislative activity giving it the authority to do so? Moreover, as mentioned in the preceding paragraph, to sanction the legitimacy of this type of organization whose mere presence and practices borders on, arguably, a form of barratry, in matters where deference to the Constitution and majority of will are at stake, how is the concept of representative governance summarily reconciled? The short answer is: *there is no reconciliation, there is only indifference.* I will suggest the query is, likely never even considered.

How can the ACLU possibly have authority to redress selective bias detrimental to the majority will when no such inanimate corpus is referenced in the Constitution? A conspicuous form of elitism in yet another example of presumed entitlement, vis-a-vis, *flat-earth idolatry.* How is it possible for the Court to indulge so blatant a bias such as this? Who, again I ask, represents the will of *The People* in circumstances both where and when fundamental constitutional issues are at stake? It clearly happens time and time again.

Simple example: Statistically the U.S. population dominantly represents itself as being a Judeo-Christian based nation (see footnote #27). How then can the minority will that there be no religious symbols on public property? Yet a president of the United States can require the U.S. Post Office to print a stamp with clear reference to Muslim traditions and simultaneously state that there is no religious preference intended? I'll offer one last example: A majority of Americans acknowledge prayer as fundamental to their faith and most official oaths include the phrase "...so help me God" as a closing affirmation. How then is prayer removed from public school on the grounds of *separation of church and state?* These types of hypocrisies call to mind Ralph Waldo Emerson's words: "What you do speaks so loud that I cannot hear what you say."

Please do not get lodged in the notion that what I'm suggesting is that the courts must adjudicate on the side of establishing a theocracy — absolutely not! However they must never render decisions that interfere in any way with its (Faith) practice, in public or in private. These just happen to be clear and conspicuous examples of the deliberate omissions of sound governance on issues of critical importance. There are many other examples of these *deliberate omissions* from the right to self-defense (that Americans no longer enjoy) to the ability to freely speak one's mind or carry personal hygiene products aboard an aircraft. From the right of an individual to fish in a stream without need of a license to the infringement upon the rights of farmers basic need of water to irrigate crops. Just a few examples of fundamental rights, regularly and increasingly infringed upon.

"REPRESENTATIVE GOVERNMENT DOES NOT RESOLVE TO GOOD GOVERNANCE IN THE ABSENCE OF A MORAL AND JUST CAUSE, IT RESOLVES ONLY THEN TO THE IMPULSE OF A SELECT GROUP!"

What becomes further proof of the impulse approach to mob rule is the application of judicial and/or legislative coercion, now absent the banner or common ideal of a moral and just people, that effectively vacate an Individuals values by imposing the bastard view of the new ideal. It is not the place or purview of the judiciary, the legislature or the president[29] to redefine the will and the identity of the very people they are charged to serve. It is only their place to protect and to be an extension of it!

"WHO THEN SPEAKS FOR THE MAJORITY WILL WHEN THE MINORITY WILLS THE OUTCOME?"

Clearly bias penetrates legislative and judicial discourse. Can we really accept the notion that a person is not defined by the ideals that are evident by his/her actions? That somehow one can mysteriously separate who they are and what their belief system is if only by/from the random action of fitting themselves with the judicial robe or carrying the banner of elected official or civil servant? The point being: There is bias in thought as it is the nature of man and his processes much as *wet is to water.* Accepting the obvious, that *wet* is the property associated with *water,* the bias must only ever be the associate will of the people and not the bias of the few.

---

29   In April of 2009, during a press conference in Turkey, Mr. Obama stated: "'One of the great strengths of the United States is we have a very large Christian population — we do not consider ourselves a Christian nation or a Jewish nation or a Muslim nation. We consider ourselves a nation of citizens who are bound by ideals and a set of values." If we parse the words, what he says is fact, however in the totality of the statement, he summarily redefines and re-invents an entire nation's historical foundation.

The ultimate perfection then, of the ideal, would be for a Jurist to resolve his personal bias toward a view that may very well not be his/her own but instead the representative will of the people as defined by the very document that binds their common ambition. Or, to extend the point to the legislative process, the rare occasion that a politician would reject the bias of a special interest group or his/her own on the same grounds. A novel thought!

It is for these reasons that I believe government must never adjudicate and/or legislate issues of conscience, but only those issues that enhance the ability of the people to ascend to their common ideal! To do anything other than this is only to enforce the divisive will of the mob over the common ideal of the people. Absent this the persistence of the contemporary notion of secularism will seal the pine box that contains the remains of a once truly fine People whose national bond was its shared values!

> "FOR SOME REASON WE SEEK TO REASON THE
> UNEXPLAINABLE AND JUSTIFY THE INEXCUSABLE."

George Washington's comments beautifully express yet another profound absolute. I heartily recommend that his Farewell Address be made a part of a mandated social studies program one which should include all grades from Kindergarten through 12th. I recommend ALL read and ponder this man's words as his effort resonates with an overwhelming love for his fellow Americans and the land he called home! On the subject of religion, the quote that soon follows is an excerpt from President Washington's final address of September, 1796. He admonishes posterity to guard against divisive tendencies with "...*indispensable supports.*" We have all, in many ways, endorsed the growth of these very tendencies by choosing to ignore the charge of our benefactor. I wonder, are we willing to pay the price of indifference? This query, as yet, has quite an *uncertain outcome.*

> *"Of all the dispositions and habits, which lead to political prosperity, Religion and Morality are indispensable supports. In vain would that man claim the tribute of Patriotism, who should labor to subvert these great pillars of human happiness, these firmest props of the duties of Men and Citizens. The mere Politician, equally with the pious man, ought to respect and to cherish them. A volume could not trace all their connections with private and public felicity. Let it simply be asked, Where is the security for property, for reputation, for life, if the sense of religious obligation desert the oaths, which are the instruments of investigation in Courts of Justice? And let us with caution indulge the supposition, that morality can be maintained without religion. Whatever may be conceded to the influence of refined education on minds of peculiar structure, reason and experience both forbid us to expect, that national morality can prevail in exclusion of religious principle."*

Do I hear an Amen? Don't worry, it is a word of Greek origin that can be thought of as a simple and *hearty affirmation!* Go ahead, nice and loud and no, the church won't summon you during a membership drive or ask for a donation. I promise, just you and I will be the only ones who will ever know. In truth, that's my great worry!

IMMIGRATION:

If ever there was one subject capable of illustrating the intended message of this entire *Series*, it would be *immigration policy*. This subject illustrates both the evidence of subverted government and the image of what will come of it. But first, a little history lesson:

> *"The name of American, which belongs to you, in your national capacity, must always exalt the just pride of Patriotism, more than any appellation derived from local discriminations. With slight shades of difference, you have the same religion, manners, habits, and political principles. You have in a common cause fought and triumphed together; the Independence and Liberty you possess are the work of joint counsels, and joint efforts, of common dangers, sufferings, and successes. In this sense it is, that your Union ought to be considered as a main prop of your liberty, and that the love of the one ought to endear to you the preservation of the other"[30].*

Separate but a Part Of is a particularly cruel dialect of thought specifically when thinking of immigration policy. This reference attempts to capture the prevailing political sentiment that somehow believes that a national policy that maintains dis-integration will evolve into or compel the adoption of a host nation's identity and ideals. Notice how precisely Mr. Washington drapes the word "American" over terms such as "same," "common," "common cause" and in his final sentence of the paragraph, "...and that the love of the one ought to endear to you the preservation of the other." Understanding this, is it truly possible for anyone to honestly believe that assimilation into the social ideal, the

---

30 George Washington's Farewell Address to the Nation. September 17, 1796. The full text of the address appears in Appendix II.

very social contract that is America, can occur simply from the mass inertia created by open border policy?

"To believe you can strengthen the ideal by disemboweling its structure is to believe in the promise of curing the disease by killing the patient! We must never extend the hand of freedom to any whose actions violate its ideals!"

There is no denying that this is a nation populated by those who have arrived on its shores from elsewhere. Further on point is some rather interesting information I've collected from a paper published by the Anthropology Outreach Office of the Smithsonian Institution. The published report indicates that there is mitochondrial DNA evidence that suggests that the ancestors of Native Americans may very well have migrated to this continent by way of the ice-fields/Alaska-Siberian land bridge. Either way, I believe it is fair to say that people, regardless of their point of origin, made their way to this part of the globe searching for a more sustainable means of subsistence. Regardless of one's historical perspective as to the settling of America, the fact remains seemingly clear that there is a noble urge that compels one to seek and perfect a better life. To escape bondage or the conscripting of ones effort in any form and join with others to assure the same or a common and beneficial outcome is a remarkable ambition. It would be a resounding demonstration of hypocrisy then to espouse the ideals of freedom whilst at the same time limiting participation. *However, as with any thing of value, there is a price and none should be exempted from paying it, to do so is to lessen its value!*

Advancing the calendar to the late 19th century and points forward, one observes that although there were demands and opportunities for supporting and populating the growing American experience, the burden was borne most particularly on industrial/commercial centers (cities) giving rise to a variety of concerns relating to health, housing, and social assimilation. Combining these with a massive increase in the numbers of those wanting to immigrate to the United States, for whatever their reasons, necessitated the development of a sound and stout immigration policy.

Regardless of one's view on immigration, there's no disputing the U.S. Census Bureau's own statistics that illustrate that under present immigration policies and related immigration rates, by year 2100 the U.S. population will grow from present estimates (2009) of nearly 300 million to nearly 600 million people. That's 300 MILLION people in less than 90 years! This is the social equivalent of the U.S. monetary policy, unchecked, unmanaged, reckless and the ultimate temptress of disaster!

> *"For happily the Government of the United States, which gives to bigotry no sanction, to persecution no assistance requires only that they who live under its protection should demean themselves as good citizens, in giving it on all occasions their effectual support."[31]*

Why does our government not address this most troubling issue? Here are four possible reasons:

1. The Two-Party System loves the conflict as it creates a transferable electoral benefit. In short, the *Two-P's* use both the fear of loss and

---

31   President George Washington 1790. It is important to consider the context of Mr. Washington's reference "...the Government of the United States....", he is referring to a constitutional government only.

the desire for beneficial gain on the part of the immigrant as a means to court votes.

2. I've no way to document the following suspicion, even after picking through various government data bases; however, try this thought on for size: Let us suggest that the widely used estimate of 20 million illegal's within our borders is actually correct. Further, let us estimate that 50% of these earn annual wages of $20,000 per year. Of this, assume that only 30% of these receive their wages by way of formal paycheck and that these wages have various federal and state "withholdings" for taxes. Using a combined "withholding" of 38% (federal income tax, Social Security, Medicare and Medicaid) this combined federal withholding would equal $22.8 billion on an annual basis. If you're the State of California, which has an 11% tax rate, this "withholding" would amount to $6 billion. Here's the question: How many of these "illegal's" do you think actually file tax returns? As you ponder the question consider this, save for the Social Security/Medicaid/Medicare portion, under the current tax code, considering the various "credits" and "exemptions," a $20,000 per year income would have little if any tax liability. Accordingly, any income tax withheld would typically be refunded. Therefore, baring the filing of a return, any wonder what happens to the revenues collected which are never returned to the taxpayer? I will address a few related issues in short order.

3. Could it be that special interests want illegal immigration to suppress or depress wages? I can think of a few reasons why there might be a beneficial reward, can't you? Perhaps I might create a simple example: Consider a large poultry processing plant that historically used domestic labor whose hourly costs, including benefits, was $23.50/hour. This labor pool is largely regional and sourced from the surrounding geographical area. The "pool" is relatively stable, therefore the company has no immediate benefit from excess or surplus labor supply which might aid suppressing wages by cycling labor with so-called "entry level" employment. The idea of lessening labor costs

still remains and as a fabulous tool for increasing profitability the temptation is quite strong. Let us accelerate the illustration just a bit: If the company can encourage the expansion of its labor pool (and by doing so slash its labor costs) by supporting an "open border policy," what side of the political aisle might be willing to accept this Employers conscientious perspective in exchange for say, a monetary/ political benefit? The line is forming! And,

4.   Could it be that the globalist prefers an open boarder policy to increasingly diminish and ultimately erase national identity? You doubt this, do you? I think one has only to make a brief study of the *social turmoil* caused by porous immigration practices in countries such as Germany, France and the United Kingdom to see the adverse effects of this type of policy. Ultimately, as we can now see by observing these three countries, the indulgence of *Selective Ideal* creates a *Conflict* leaving few, if any, pain-free options. Particularly if one of the preferred options is to undo the damage.

> "INDULGENCE ONLY CREATES THE EXPECTATIONS
> OF ADDICTIONS WHOSE DEMANDS ANCHOR AND
> CONSTRICT WITH THE RESOLVE OF A VISE!"

In many ways the government's negligence in faithfully resolving the immigration issue is wholly consistent with the globalist's views. What follows is a series of parenthetical comments; throughout your review consider each not only as it relates to the immigration issue but also as a benefit to one holding a global agenda.

BORDER FREE:

When grappling with the unwieldy nature of immigration, one discovers that it is nearly impossible to avoid the discussion of national security. I'm at a loss for any reasonable explanation as to why the federal government has maintained so casual a regard for adequate border security. Clearly one can assign immigration management as a constitutional mandate and not withstanding the frequent appeals of Southwestern border states, the matter receives only the classic "nod and wink" of the *federales*. Even in the rare instance that legislation is actually introduced once the "back slapping" has subsided and the cameras are tuned to a new *love-child*, the politicians either gut the funding requirements or fail to pass the enabling legislation.

It may also be important to consider the border issue in the broader terms of trade agreements such as NAFTA/CAFTA etc. These trade agreements have made it very difficult to conduct sound border policy particularly when matters of commerce are at issue. It should come as no surprise that the increase in cross-border drug traffic has accompanied reduced border oversight. Three pertinent quotes follow:

- "The debate over immigration should not be whether it makes for a much larger population — without question it does. The debate over immigration should also not be whether it has a large impact on the aging of society — without question it does not. The central question this study raises and that Americans must answer is what costs and benefits come with having a much larger population and a more densely settled country."[32]

- "The growth of transnational gangs has been a dangerous side effect of our failure to control the U.S.-Mexico border and our tolerance for high levels of illegal immigration."[33]

---

32   Center for Immigration Studies, Steven Camarota 8/07

33   U.S. Dept of Justice, National Gang Threat Assessment 2005

- "So as the politicians argue about border fences and amnesty, they are missing the bigger picture: the harmful impact of large-scale settlement of all kinds of immigrants, whether legal or illegal, skilled or unskilled, temporary or permanent, European or Latin or Asian or African. Modern America has simply outgrown immigration, and we must end it before it cripples us."[34]

CHEAP LABOR:

The assertion that illegal immigration policy is justified to provide labor for "jobs Americans won't do" is simply not supported by the facts. Further, I find the premise's inference nakedly vulgar particularly if the motive then becomes to provide cheap labor on the backs of those who do not possess the means to advance beyond that standing. In effect, it promotes the establishment of a *slave* or *peasant* class evidenced by one of many such programs where public schools teach bi-lingual/native language/immersion programs which further inculcates the disintegration of the American fabric. Further, it serves to perpetuate economic caste and suppress the individual's ability to improve his status, economic or otherwise. When one considers the devastating economic consequences of "off shoring" all of the most valuable components of a functional *wealth creating economy*, not only does this reality prohibit economic advancement, it redefines the traditional American culture into two distinct classification: *Those who have and those who do not!* Consider the following few points:

---

34   The New Case Against Immigration, Legal and Illegal by Mark Krikorian June 2008

- "There is no evidence of a labor shortage, especially at the bottom end of the labor market where immigrants are most concentrated. If there was, wages, benefits and employment should all be increasing fast, the opposite of what has been happening. Employment has declined significantly for the less-educated."[35]

- "In our analysis of the March 2007 Current Population Survey, we estimate that there are approximately 11.3 million illegal aliens living in the United States. Our estimate for the number of illegal's included in the 2000 CPS is 7.3 million. This means that the illegal-alien population grew by four million between 2000 and 2007."[36]

- In February, 2008, the Senate Stimulus Bill was being considered and if passed would contain about $104 billion in new government funding for construction projects; the goal being to create jobs for unemployed Americans. *The Bill does not contain any prohibitions* on employment for Illegal applicants and if one were to consider the Governments stated estimates of 2 Million newly created jobs, one might find the following information of interest: "Consistent with other research, the Center Immigration Studies has previously estimated that 15 percent of construction workers are illegal immigrants. This means that about 300,000 of the construction jobs created by the Senate stimulus could go to illegal aliens (15 percent of 2 million)."[37]

---

35   Immigration's Impact on American Workers May 9, 2007 by Steven A. Camarota Director of Research Center for Immigration Studies.

36   Center for Immigration Studies: "Immigration: Summary April 2009

37   Center for Immigration Studies: Steven Camarota Director of Research, February, 2009

DIS-INTEGRATION:

A much larger issue accompanies failed immigration policy. The issue manifests itself in so many tragic ways. The social and economic dysfunction is pervasive, as are its burdens. Not only are the following points alarming, but more importantly, we can no longer turn a blind eye to their cost in human degradation:

- The current immigration policy has served to segment our national ideals. This policy promotes social and economic disintegration by creating and perpetuating a subculture that sustains racial bias, which in turn further fractures the assimilation process. Viewing the matter simply on the issue of language is to observe how far from reason we have strayed.

- "The aliens arrested under Operation Community Shield collectively represent a significant menace to the public. The vast majority (80 percent) have committed serious crimes in addition to immigration violations and a large number (40 percent) have violent criminal histories."[38]

- "We estimate that 57 percent of the illegal alien population comes from Mexico, 11 percent from Central America, 9 percent from East Asia, 8 percent from South America, and Europe and the Caribbean account for 4 percent. Of all immigrants from Mexico, 55 percent are illegal; for Central Americans it is 47 percent; and it is 33 percent for South Americans. It should be noted that these estimates only

---

38 U.S. Dept of Justice, National Gang Threat Assessment 2005

include illegal aliens captured by the March CPS (Current Population Survey), not those missed by the survey."[39]

- "The National Research Council estimated that immigrant households create a net fiscal burden (taxes paid minus services used) on all levels of government of $20.2 billion annually."[40]

- "The Center for Immigration Studies (CIS) estimates that in 2002 illegal alien households imposed costs of $26 billion on the federal government and paid $16 billion in federal taxes, creating an annual net fiscal deficit of $10.4 billion at the federal level, or $2,700 per household. Among the largest federal costs, were Medicaid ($2.5 billion); treatment for the uninsured ($2.2 billion); food assistance programs such as food stamps, WIC (Women, Infants & Children), and free school lunches ($1.9 billion); the federal prison/ court systems ($1.6 billion); and federal aid to schools ($1.4 billion)."[41]

- "The Center for Immigration Studies estimates that state and local governments spend some $4 billion a years to provide health care to illegal aliens and their U.S.-born children and $20 to $24 billion to educate children from illegal alien households. Many of the costs associated with illegal aliens are due to their U.S.-born children who have American citizenship. Thus, barring illegal aliens themselves

39   Senate Amnesty Could Strain Welfare System: Steven Camarota June 2007

40   Immigration's Impact on Public Coffers August 24, 2006, Steven A. Camarota Director of Research, Center for Immigration Studies

41   Immigration's Impact on Public Coffers August 24, 2006, Steven A. Camarota Director of Research, Center for Immigration Studies

from programs will have little impact on costs." [42]   *It is precisely for this reason the abuse of the 14th Amendment needs to be brought to an end.*

- "There are now some 400,000 children born to illegal-alien mothers each year in the United States, accounting for almost one in 10 births in the country. Of all births to immigrants, 39 percent were to mothers without a high school education, and among illegal's it was more than 65 percent."[43]

- "There is a common but mistaken belief that welfare programs are only for those who don't work. Actually, the welfare system is designed to provide low-wage workers, or more often their children, things like food, assistance and health care. It is the presence of their U.S.-born children coupled with their low education levels that explains why so many immigrant households use the welfare system. Many of the welfare costs described above are due to the presence of U.S.-born children, who are awarded U.S. citizenship at birth. Thus, the prohibition on new immigrants using some welfare programs makes little difference because their U.S.-citizen children will continue to be eligible. We estimate that nearly 400,000 children are born to illegal aliens each year."[44]

---

42   Immigration's Impact on Public Coffers August 24, 2006, Steven A. Camarota Director of Research, Center for Immigration Studies

43   National Center for Health Statistics: *Births to Immigrations in America, 1970 to 2002*

44   Immigration's Impact on Public Coffers August 24, 2006, Steven A. Camarota Director of Research, Center for Immigration Studies

HEALTH CONCERNS:

In recent years we have seen a resurgence of various diseases that have been nonexistent in this country for many years. Owing to both our nonexistent immigration and self-destructive trade policies we have invited alarming rates of infectious diseases. Either through increased importation of food products or from Illegal Immigrants, the heath threats are nothing short of alarming! Consider the following points:

- "Many illegal's who cross our borders have tuberculosis. That disease had largely disappeared from America, thanks to excellent hygiene and powerful modern drugs such as isoniazid and rifampin. TB.s swift, deadly return now is lethal for about 60 percent of those infected because of new Multi-Drug Resistant Tuberculosis (MDRTB). Until recently MDR-TB was endemic to Mexico. This *Mycobacterium tuberculosis* is resistant to at least two major antitubercular drugs."[45]

- "Chagas disease, also called American trypanosomiasis or kissing bug disease is transmitted by the reduviid bug, which prefers to bite the lips and face. The protozoan parasite that it carries, *Trypanosoma cruzi*, infects 18 million people annually in Latin America and causes 50,000 deaths. This disease also infiltrates America's blood supply. Chagas affects blood transfusions and transplanted organs. No cure exists. Hundreds of blood recipients may be silently infected." [46]

45　Illegal Aliens and American Medicine: Madeleine Pelner Cosman, PhD, Esq. : Journal of American Physicians and Surgeons Volume 10 Number 1 Spring 2005:

46　ibid

- "Leprosy, Hansen's disease, was so rare in America that in 40 years only 900 people were afflicted. Suddenly, in the past three years America has more than 7,000 cases of leprosy. Leprosy now is endemic to northeastern states because illegal aliens and other immigrants brought leprosy from India, Brazil, the Caribbean, and Mexico." [47]

- "Dengue fever is exceptionally rare in America, though common in Ecuador, Peru, Vietnam, Thailand, Bangladesh, Malaysia, and Mexico. Recently there was a virulent outbreak of dengue fever in Webb County, Texas, which borders Mexico. Though dengue is usually not a fatal disease, dengue hemorrhagic fever routinely kills." [48]

- "Polio was eradicated from America, but now reappears in illegal immigrants, as do intestinal parasites. Malaria was obliterated, but now is re-emerging in Texas. About 4,000 children under age five annually in America develop fever, red eyes, strawberry tongue, and acute inflammation of their coronary arteries and other blood vessels because of the infectious malady called Kawasaki disease. Many suffer heart attacks and sudden death." [49]

- "Hepatitis A, B, and C, are resurging. Asians number 4 percent of Americans, but account for more than half of Hepatitis B cases. Why inoculate American newborns for Hepatitis B when most infected persons are Asians?" [50]

---

47   ibid
48   ibid
49   ibid
50   ibid

Whatever one labels the inertial force that lies just behind the emerald curtain, whether it be globalism, predation or just plain neglect, the fact is this country cannot afford the social, environmental, systemic and sovereignty costs associated with the current immigration policy. The political class is, in effect, treating this country as a dumping ground in exchange for the entitlement of special interests, whatever or whomever they may be. In place of these practices, why is the consequential burden not placed on the countries of origin? Perhaps this approach is simply just another indicator of the much-heralded process of "making the world safe for democracy" or its *bastard-child* pitch, "economic interests?" Just curious!

"MORE OF BAD DOESN'T MAKE THE BAD BETTER,
IT JUST MAKE WHATEVER IT IS, WORSE!"

A clear distinction needs to be made between what constitutes the right to citizenship and by what means, i.e., *immigration policy*, it may occur. As we can see from the material above, there is no either/or when it comes to principles which when violated bear clear and significant consequences. Neither does the political charade of "worker visa," "temporary visa" or any of the proposed variants suspend these consequences.

"WE CAN NOT EXPECT THE IDEA OF *SEPARATE BUT A
PART OF* TO BE A FUNCTIONAL IMMIGRATION POLICY. IT
VOIDS THE REQUIREMENT OF ASSIMILATION AND THE
CONVERGENCE OF ALL PARTS UPON A COMMON IDEAL."

As a nation we simply must grasp that whatever the compelling force, the effects of these social/entitlement issues and the various means by which they are arbitrarily promoted serve only to destabilize the very fabric of the United States. This occurs by the willful fracturing of its structure and the weakening of its national ideals.

> *"The policy or advantage of immigration taking place in a body (I mean the settling of them in a body) may be much questioned; for, by so doing, they retain the Language, habits and principles (good or bad) which they bring with them. Whereas by an intermixture with our people, they, or their descendants, get assimilated to our customs, measures and laws: in a word, soon become one people."* [51]

If we do not tender for *recognition* and *allegiance* the principles that have defined this nation and its promise then we present no measure by which any immigrant may be bound. If there is no principle that compels the duty of allegiance, then by what reason do we rightfully expect to be a nation of free and just people? If there is no *thing* or *ideal* for one to ascend to and onto which we might focus our duty, our honor and our industry, then the promise is but a shell which bears the shame of hollow intention.

> *"If they look back through this history to trace their connection with those days [of the Founding] by blood, they find they have none, they cannot carry themselves back into that glorious epoch and make themselves feel that they are part of us, but when they look through that old Declaration of Independence they find that those old men say that 'We hold these truths to be self-evident, that all men are created equal,' and then they feel that that moral sentiment taught in that day evidences their relation to those men, that it is the father of all moral principle*

---

51   George Washington: letter to John Adams, November 15, 1794

in them, and that they have a right to claim it as though they were blood of the blood, and flesh of the men who wrote that Declaration, (loud and long continued applause) and so they are. That is the electric cord in that Declaration that links the hearts of patriotic and liberty-loving men together, that will link those patriotic hearts as long as the love of freedom exists in the minds of men throughout the world.[52]

For all who would claim to be American, it is not sufficient to simply claim the title, it is not sufficient to claim citizenship and it is not sufficient to claim lineage or entitlement by birth. But more so, it is to understand the true value of the Declaration of Independence and the Constitution of the United States. *Most* importantly to appreciate, understand and hold sacred the nobility of its purpose and the necessity of which that made its *Ideals* worth fighting and dying for!

"YES, IT TRULY IT IS A MELTING POT. THE ONLY PROBLEM IS THAT IT'S THE POT THAT IS MELTING!"

---

52 Abraham Lincoln: July 10, 1858. A speech, dwarfed by the epoch of his Gettysburg Address, still reverberates with his unique form. In his use of the word "they" he refers to the immigrant population who has no direct relationship to residency at the time of the country's birth.

Legal/Election Practices:

Moving as I am to bring closure to the subject of *The Policy of Conflict and Selective Ideals,* the presentation would be incomplete if I failed to comment on two specific issues. I've merged numerous observations into what, in effect, becomes a hybrid of topics; however, I am certain the complicit issues are easily identifiable. They will be quite familiar and, if they are not, they soon will.

Some time ago I received an email from a dear friend. The email being circulated was a political commentary relating to proposed legislation for the "bailout" of various financial enterprises as well as the issue of "executive bonuses." As most Americans understand these legislative adventures do not serve the American economy; more importantly, they do not serve the American people. We know that, we understand that and we are becoming more and more deeply troubled by the slight of hand gambit. Preferring to follow-up his email by phone, Don called and without so much as a hello, here is how the call began: "So, what do you make of this mess? How is this possible? How do these people get elected? Am I the only one who sees what is happening?" I answered his question in the following way:

"IT IS POSSIBLE BECAUSE THEY PRACTICE GOVERNMENT LIKE THEY PRACTICE LAW. NOT FROM THE POSITION OF CONVERGING UPON THE IDEAL, BUT TO ARBITRATE DOWN TO THE LOWEST POSSIBLE COMMON DENOMINATOR."

And,

"THEY GET ELECTED OR REELECTED BECAUSE THE
SYSTEM, AS IT IS PRACTICED, PREFERS TO PRESENT THE
FAVOR OF THE FAVORED AS THE ONLY CHOICE!"

I also told him, "No, you are not alone, you are like me and millions like us, who are the mass the system ignores because they believe you are sufficiently shackled and no longer possess value they've not already attached. *This belief will prove to be their undoing!*"

Now it is true that there are some wonderful folks holding elected office; however, if one recalls my crustacean metaphor from earlier on in these writings, these critters are not allowed out of the bucket. Well, at least not long enough to have any effect.

If the framers of the Constitution had intended career politicians they would have, as is the case with Supreme Court justices, provided for life tenure. As there is no provision made (in the Constitution) for this, I see no reason for these extended retreats to be permitted and far too many reasons for why they should be excised. When one considers the failure rate of these resident life forms, well let's just leave the point open for you to complete the thought. If the legislative process were to be practiced as a form of arbitration (compromise) then the founders would have most likely accommodated this intention with a slight variation on the 10th Amendment. It may even have appeared as follows:

"...the powers not delegated to the United States by the Con-
stitution and ignoring prohibitions by the States and with

concurrent indifference to the People, may be presumed and compromised at will."[53]

Still, time and time again I hear the phrase, "Politics is the art of compromise" which has most certainly become the practice of our system of government. It is not considered as a prohibition but a fact of life in the common practices of *high* government. If we accept for the moment that a *compromise* implies something *less than* then it follows that what one has accomplished (by compromise) is to settle for some *thing* even less than that! In other words, you've not only surrendered your position, but you've also surrender your principles. Holding the image of the federal legislative process in mind, I'm not clear where there's cause for celebration when one hears (spoken with dubious and duplicitous acclaim): *We've arrived at a bipartisan compromise!*

"BIPARTISAN COMPROMISE IS CLAIMING DEFEAT WHEN THE ALTERNATIVE — PREFERABLY, TO HAVE DONE NOTHING AT ALL — WOULD HAVE BEEN SUCCESS IN ITS PUREST FORM!"

Yes, it is true, we make compromises in business transactions, we make compromises on what we eat for dinner, we may even make compromises on the type of car we drive by selecting a hybrid. However, in the area of governance, particularly in the constitutional republic form, there must never be this type of practiced arbitration. I'm often left to wonder why simply doing nothing is never even considered as an option! Where is the American in the political concourse who says,

---

53   The modified portion of the 10th Amendment to the U.S. Constitution actually appears as follows: "…the powers not delegated to the United States by the Constitution, nor prohibited by it to the States, are reserved to the States respectively, or to the people." I pray the founding fathers will forgive my messing with it.

"No, we don't do that to the Constitution, you do that in the lavatory!" Why is going back and starting anew or crafting legislation consistent with the ideal so elusive a concept? The whole purpose of the bicameral, for that matter, tricameral (if one includes the judiciary) form of government is to be a check and balance, with the overriding ideal being that which is defined by the Constitution. Why the rush to mediocrity, or even worse, failure?

> "IN THE GAME OF POLITICAL COMPROMISE, ADVERSE OR
> OPPOSING OPINION BECOMES AN UNWILLING ACCOMPLICE
> SERVING ONLY TO OBSCURE WHAT BECOMES THE PROMISE!"

Yes, even in the judicial selection process the two-party system of *Conflict and Selective Ideal* policy adversely penetrated the process. Judgeships are controlled by political intention which splinters the interests of the Constitution and thereby the interests of the people. The system selects justices it believes reflect its biased perspective and not the underlying principle that a judge should be entirely unbiased with regard to his personal ambitions and completely biased only toward the Constitution.

I'm reminded of the confirmation process for Supreme Court Chief Justice Roberts. I marveled at the time consumed by one senator in particular who repeatedly queried the nominee on the issue of *stare decisis*[54] and their disposition, most notably, regarding the senator's personal preference towards the Court's decision on Roe v. Wade. Whatever the intentions, ultimately this senator's contribution to the confirmation process revealed to me the near-uniform preference for preserving

---

54   Stare Decisis: in Latin it means "to stand by things decided". It is, in effect, a legal doctrine that preserves, as precedent, a prior judicial decision.

errors in judgment over assuring and insuring systemic deference to the Constitution. After all, compromise is justice too. No?

I believe the process has drawn itself, deliberately, into the realm of the *vague and obscure* and these, my friends, have only one known cure — the restoration of clarity. The focal point of restoration must center about the fundament principles whose focus is secured only upon the legitimate interests of the people as expressed in the Constitution and most certainly not those expressed through the lens of unopposed social, political, economic or legislative bias.

"WHEN THE POLITICAL SYSTEM SHIFTS THE BALANCE AWAY FORM THE CONSTITUTIONAL PRINCIPLES, WHO THEN IS LEFT TO ASSERT YOUR CONSTITUTIONAL RIGHTS? CORRECT, NOT A ONE!"

States rights provides yet another example of orchestrated bias of *Policy of Conflict* and *Selective Ideals.* Though this is not the only possible example, others being minimum wage laws, various interstate commerce laws, gun laws, hate crime legislation, etc., it is the most divisive and most conspicuous. I speak of various federal impositions on individual rights specifically guarded from interference, most specifically, religion, with however, a slight twist to further illustrate the point. (Note: Yes, I frequently illustrate examples using *religion* but not from the position of being a religious zealot. I use it precisely because it is the most conspicuous and most vulnerable to attack. It has also become one with the fewest political and legal advocates. For this reason, it is the most effective example from which to emphasize how far government has wondered from sound practices.)

In all honesty, I find the freedoms of speech, assembly (sometimes thought of a freedom of association) and the right of privacy more frequently assaulted. Still, my observations can be made most efficiently through the lens of *religion*. To that end, consider the manner in which one's personal religious views or moral compass is affected through the conflict and bias of the political system's selective ideals. Take for example, a politician whose political or state interests are furthered by presenting legislation preferred by mob interests, which in turn, will have national consequences. Think of it!

Take for example, so-called "hate crime" legislation, which is motivated by a vigilant and divisive minority able to coerce a weak-minded federal government into passing legislation that not only silences one's personal beliefs and opinions, but also imposes the force of law upon one's right to freedom of speech, assembly/association and religious convictions. Consider the following example: A pastor, or any believer for that matter, will be subject to criminal prosecution for professions of faith or espousing of doctrines which another may find offensive. Have we lost our MINDS? Expressing one's beliefs or opinions is now a hate crime?

What in the name of puffed-rice does anyone think was the reason behind the First Amendment in the first place? To protect polite speech? NO, the First Amendment isn't there to protect "let's make nice speech," it's there to protect the rights of the person whose speaking makes your blood boil! Freedom of religion means just what it says. Freedom to PRACTICE your religion, even if your religion is to practice no religion at all! Folks, this is high-diving into the shallow end of an empty pool and it doesn't get any more absurd than this. Well, as a matter of fact, yes, it does.

"FREEDOM OF SPEECH ENABLES, IN PRACTICE, THE FREEDOM TO SPEAK! WITHOUT THE COMPANION OF OPINION THERE IS NONE!"

My entire point is to make clear that it is your right not only to offend, but also to be offended. It is not the right of government to interfere, in ANY way, with these rights. Doing so, in any form, is not the actions of a representative form of government. I'm reminded, as you should be, too, of a certain pledge:

"I PLEDGE ALLEGIANCE, TO THE FLAG, OF THE UNITED STATES OF AMERICA AND TO THE REPUBLIC FOR WHICH IT STANDS, ONE NATION, UNDER GOD, INDIVISIBLE, WITH LIBERTY AND JUSTICE FOR ALL."

Party politics automatically divides people and amplifies disintegration by imposing the interests of one over another. Doing so is clearly not consistent with the idea of a one "indivisible" people. As is also the case with immigration or commerce, the allure of the United States must be, at the very minimum, equal to one's allegiance to the unifying ideal, the common principle and not to the nation from whence the immigrant came nor the notion upon which an individual personal compass navigates.

I'm reminded of how my fourth grade teacher, Miss Tucci, dealt with her students when familiarity with our desk mates made for a dysfunctional class; she'd reassign desks. What a splendid idea for Congress; perhaps the more appropriate option is to simply send them home.

JUSTICE AND SELECTIVE IDEALS:

"WE ARE NOT PERFECTING THE IDEAL OF JUSTICE, WE
ARE ONLY EVER PERFECTING THE PRACTICE OF LAW."

In order to determine the validity of any law or proposed legislation should there not be a construct, i.e., a means or measure by which said law must or may be judged in deference to the Constitution? Without this function, as we have seen, nearly any law can be passed with absolutely no regard to constitutional prohibitions. We have seen the consequences of these acts of omission many times throughout our nation's history and with chilling effects. I will cover a select few of these events later on in this *series*, each are iconic in their lasting effect upon this nation.

For now though, let me introduce two instances where the government clearly steps outside the boundaries of the Constitution in particularly troublesome ways.

- Any/all legislation possessing administrative "conveniences" that are not clearly defined by said legislation. This approach leaves to the bureaucratic process the creation of processes (rules and regulations) that in effect, have the full force and affect of law. These notoriously occur at all levels of government and occur outside the conventional regiments of legislative, not to mention legal, oversight. They give rise to all sorts of intrusive excesses from the various trade agreements, the Endangered Species Act right on down to local zoning and building codes. These types of regulations provide no representative discretion or opposition and are completely corrosive to the ideals of representative government.

- Judicial or *bench* actions on the part of the courts. Again, as in the former, these are *decisions* that occur outside the legislative process and are purely discretionary. It is one thing to render a decision based upon the law and within the boundaries of relevant precedence, it is quite another to establish what in essence become a rule of law simply by, in effect, judicial decree.

In any and all cases,

"It is essential to the preservation of the rights of every individual, his life, liberty, property, and character, that there be an impartial interpretation of the laws, and administration of justice."[55]

The Constitution specifically states that it is the "supreme law of the land."[56] Consequently, it would seem appropriate that the U.S. Supreme Court, as the ultimate arbiter, should be the means (as it was intended) by which the process would be perfected. The idea is further supported by the premise that prescribes independence of this court as well as its jurists, which must be preserved as sacrosanct.

"The complete independence of the courts of justice is peculiarly essential in a limited Constitution. By a limited Constitution, I understand one which contains certain specified exceptions to the legislative authority; such, for instance, as that it shall pass

---

55   The Report of a Constitution or Form of Government, for the Commonwealth of Massachusetts - John Adams, Revolutionary Writings, 1763. Emphasis added by C. Greco.

56   U.S. Constitution, Article 6, Paragraph 2.

no bills of attainder, no ex post facto laws, and the like. Limitations of this kind can be preserved in practice no other way than through the medium of courts of justice, whose duty it must be to declare all acts contrary to the manifest tenor of the Constitution void. Without this, all the reservations of particular rights or privileges would amount to nothing.[57]

From this reason if no other, there must be "judicial review" of legislative actions particularly on the federal level. The argument that there is no mandate provided by the Constitution accommodating the idea of judicial review is based purely on the bias of those who make this assertion. The opposing idea is that any "judicial review" should rest exclusively in the "trial by jury" provisional structure. The extension of this theory being that the beneficial affect of "judicial review" would occur as a result of the public will.

Consider first the question of "who" was consulted in the crafting of the law (whichever one that is in question) in the first place? Clearly, if it was the will of the people then there would be no argument; however, if the political will was otherwise, then who, absent the Supreme Court, would protest in favor of the will of the people so expressed or defined by the U.S. Constitution? The answer is quite simple; *no* such entity is able to independently address the issue.

Opponents of judicial review are more interested in the preservation of their standing as practitioners of the law than as advocates of its perfection.

---

57   Alexander Hamilton: Federalist Paper # 78, June 14, 1788.

"We, I hope, shall adhere to our republican government and keep it to its original principles by narrowly watching it." [58]

Consider the WTO/GAATD/NAFT (various trade treaties) disasters as an example, in practical terms, of why and how this approach (absent judicial review) fails so miserably. These treaties clearly were promulgated not by the will of the people but by the political will of vested interests. Further, they breach several constitutional principles, most notably the constitutional principle of sovereignty.

The opponents of judicial review would leave the correction of this error in judgment to the legislative process, whereby congress would propose an amendment or the states would convene a Constitutional Convention. *I trust you are seeing the complete lunacy of expecting this to occur, but let us continue for a moment or two more.* Considering that Congress affirmed these treaties in 1995 and despite the complicit subordination of U.S. sovereignty, including but not limited to its economic, social and legal apparatus and the ill effects of having done so, there has yet to be any successful challenge to their passage. So much for the validity of the opponents' of judicial review and their position!

Let me attempt to restate the issue this way. If legislation is passed by Congress that is structurally unconstitutional, again, absent the Supreme Court striking it down as being so, how likely is it that the legislature would be willing to put its constitutionality to the test by promulgating a constitutional amendment that will affirm, or at least call in to question, its unconstitutionality? Even more, absent the political will or means of the people to prevent the law's passage in the

---

first place, how likely is it that the people will be able to compel their state governments, three-fourths of them, to achieve the same resolution through a Constitutional Convention? Your answer should be: *Not likely!*

> *"There is no position which depends on clearer principles, than that every act of a delegated authority, contrary to the tenor of the commission under which it is exercised, is void. No legislative act, therefore, contrary to the Constitution, can be valid. To deny this, would be to affirm, that the deputy is greater than his principle; that the servant is above his master; that the representatives of the people are superior to the people themselves; that men acting by virtue of powers, may do not only what their powers do not authorize, but what they forbid."[59]*

I surely do hope you rejoice in the substance of Alexander Hamilton's message which needs no clarification or amplification from me.

ELECTION: CONFLICT OF IDEALS:

Many of Abraham Lincoln's comments have been recorded and I find the simplicity of his eloquence equaled only by his profound wisdom. History records past attempts at democratic rule, the most notable being the Greeks and the Romans and like others before him schooled in classical studies, Lincoln also observed a common theme among these cultures' demise. Mr. Lincoln's comment, which follows, describes this resonant theme quite well:

---

59   Alexander Hamilton, Federalist Paper # 78, June 14, 1788

"America will never be destroyed from the outside. If we falter and lose our freedoms, it will be because we destroyed ourselves."

Only when honored, preserved and practiced can the republican form of democratic government succeed. Democracies, present and past, ultimately fail because they inevitable bend to tyrannical bias. The republican form's distinction is characterized by a fundamental principle that I think is best evidenced by the ideal "the will of the people." As mentioned throughout, "the will of the people" is not the bias of a few or coercion from the mob, the courts, a legislature or a president, but the conformance by all of these entities, of and unto an overriding ideal that is common to all! Consider this:

"As I would not be a slave, so I would not be a master. This expresses my idea of democracy." [60]

Implicit in this statement is a fundamental ideal of the republican form of government. It is the "high road" course sought by people of character and courage through the expression not only of the implied ability that their station may entitle, but also the implicit reservation that provides and enforces the restraint and prohibition of imposition! This is the beauty and ideal of the republican form of government, honored, preserved and practiced! *To neither succumb to the mob who would preserve or invoke their will, nor to bend the ideal to accommodate their ambition!*

---

60   Abraham Lincoln: 1858

"The demonstration of noble grace is not announced or even compelled, it is the silent messenger of your action when the need is greatest and one appears unannounced."

The honor, preservation and practice of this simple principle is the only barrier that exists between republicanism and any/all forms of tyranny! Unfortunately, it is the trust implicit in this ideal, conveyed by the people to their elected officials, *that is so frequently violated!*

Nonetheless, one would hope to cleanse the system of political and coercive bias through the election process — one would hope! However,

"To what benefit is the ideal when not a one speaks the language of its virtue and none bear witness to its value by their practices!"

Please recall my response to the inquiry of a friend; I believe one will find it relevant to this discussion.

"They get elected or reelected because the system, as it is practiced, prefers to present the favor of the favored as the only choice!"

The *Conflict of Ideals* is perpetuated by an election process that, in my opinion, has run afoul. It is hopelessly askew of republican ideals and in practice perfects the bias of intentions contrary to the will of the people. Instead of the candidates presenting themselves as proponents of the ideals of republicanism, they attest instead to their willingness to infringe on these ideals with the bias of party affiliation. Instead of the candidates inspiring the voter by championing the cause of freedom and liberty, they entice the voter with promises of further impositions.

The divisive nature of the present two-party system serves to perpetuate the system as it is. It does this through a form of *nepotism by default* or by *mandate*. The election process is structured to favor the incumbent and shields this politician from the consequences of his/her measured performance and thus secures the inherent nature of the two-party bias toward *Conflict and Selective Ideal*. One day you're the hammer, the next day you're the nail! I refer to this as political inertia; the party that sells its bias more effectively to a fractured and disoriented people *wins!* Again, not performance based, but political bias based! The premier example of this system in action is seen in the case of the *party-switch* politician who fears failing support of his/her party jumps ship in favor of the dominant force. So much for conviction!

It's also interesting to consider that when the measure of performance is the measure of mediocrity, the politician has not real need to excel in the area of expressing or promoting republican principles. When there is no opposition, when there is no choice, when there is no compelling ideal upon which to aspire, it seems *nothing* will suit the outcome just fine.

The system developed a very efficient means by which it could neuter the "will of the people" as well as the mandates of the republican form of government. This occurs by the illusion of partisanship; not parti-sanship toward the ideals of government, but instead to the ideals of the party's interpretation, or bias, as to what and how those ideals are to be defined. Then, as if a matter of fact, the voter is left with the notion that the means or access to the ideals of good government, as an expression of their will, can only be achieved by the options (Republican or

Democratic party) provided. The system then, by default, has just effectively herded the *sheople* down one or the other of two manufactured corridors. Thus, unknowingly, not only has the will of the people been fractured, but the great lie of two-party politics and its means has been made a near inseparable component of the systemic bias.

Once elected, in many cases the trappings, temptations and endemic forces of elected office assume the role of compass that conviction may have otherwise occupied. With no clear commitment to an assured outcome, the voter, now worn and discouraged, has only the choice offered, and as we know, that is no choice at all!

The system restricts access to the principle of sound governance simply by domination. The policies established for financial support are laughable at best, deceptive in form and function at their absolute worst. Terms such as "hard" and "soft" campaign contributions are structured in such a way not only to garner financial support, but actually to conceal their sources. The maze of funding sources from individuals, political action committees, national and regional party groups/affiliates, non-profits, party caucuses, lobbyist etc. is a *who's who* of vested interests. It should come as no surprise that no sooner is a candidate elected than the realities of reelection set in and the system ramps up to spend immense amounts of time and resources to prepare for the next round. This begets the cycle of contemporary politics, always with an eye toward what pays and what pays is the influence that is garnered in exchange for access to the halls where influence is peddled and outcome is measured in reward!

Reviewing the Federal Election Commission data it is interesting to note that a candidate for the Senate or House of Representatives should expect to spend four to eight million dollars for a job that pays

$174,000 per year. It would seem to me that the price for admission should be more of an admonition than a right of passage.

> "WE OUGHT TO BE MORE MINDFUL OF CAMPAIGNS WHO FUND PROMISES AND LESS ON CAMPAIGN RHETORIC. IT IS THE FORMER WHICH, ONCE THE SUN HAS RETIRED, WILL SEE THE LIGHT OF DAY. THE LATER WILL QUIETLY BECOME ANONYMOUS!"

I expect one will be tempted to consider my words overly simplistic and I've admonished myself with great intention as this is as I intended. There are far too many reasons as to the *why's* and *how's* the system has become what it is to be explored herein. However, I will rest on a simple anecdotal reference: If one can manage to remove or camouflage the spots on a dog, it won't change the fact that the animal is still a dog.

The fact of the matter is this: If there are two parties then, in a republican from of government, they can only be defined as follows:

- The party that is for and supports the republican form of government where the will of the people, as expressed by its Constitution and supporting documents, is the standard that is kept.

Or,

- The party that believes in the aristocratic right of ascension, the entitled elite where there is no recognized mandate known as the "will of the people."

If we accept these in their basic form as the only two alternatives, either version being a republic or tyranny, once all of the trappings are removed, then which party would one assign allegiance too? Whichever your choice, make no mistake, as practiced, partisan politics is in complete opposition to your intention. As it is, it splinters principles of sound governance into an either/or scenario and I trust we can agree that the political animal should never be let off the leash that binds and draws him nearer to, not further from, the trust that is bestowed upon him/her by *The People.*

A Summary on the Policy of Conflict and Selective Ideals

IN PREPARING THIS MATERIAL for the entire series I often found myself asking again and again, the very same question: What was the cause of the systemic dysfunction and as well, the source of all the passionate expressions of so many with whom I've come in contact with over the past few years. I've spent many hours in thoughtful reflections, hours reading periodicals, historical references, listening to commentators as well the many answers from those who tolerated my seemingly endless inquiries.

Yes indeed, the material was immense and I would digest and filter each piece looking for the answer, the common and elusive thread and suddenly, as if it was there all along, it appeared! What I discovered was that the answer was not so much in the form of a resolution or my discovering the identity of one simple omission or key ingredient; no, it revealed itself as yet another question. I'll address my discovery in a moment; however, to provide a greater degree of context, indulge me as I reintroduction a passage offered from earlier in this volume:

"THE PEOPLE'S GREATEST TORMENT IS NEITHER FEAR
NOR SO MUCH AS THE ABANDONMENT OF THEIR MORAL

COMPASS. NO, IT IS MORE LIKELY THAT IT IS THEIR SENSE OF DUTY AND HONOR THAT HAS BEEN CORRUPTED BY THE COMPLETE AND UTTER DISBELIEF THAT THEIR OWN HAVE SO WILLINGLY AND SO RECKLESSLY VIOLATED THEIR TRUST!"

This passage is a critical centerpiece in expressing my revelation. What I discovered was not conspicuously written in text or even spoken, but it was there in the maze of information and on the faces of the many people with whom I spoke. I suspect it may be for you, the reader, the same unspoken thought as well. *Why?*

Why is a powerful point of order in this instance, particularly because this unique outcome becomes the determining factor as it occurs not from the position of limitations or scarcity of opportunity, but from an environment that offers so much opportunity, so much abundance, so much promise! It is the only element capable of accommodating the expressions of genius that if released, fully, promises a future that will dwarf man's greatest achievements to date!

Yet, *why* does not full explain the matter at hand either; it requires one last step to the *what* that lies just behind the *why.* The result was two clear distinctions: (1) What was the "promise" of government? And (2) How does the government interpret what this *promise* is and to what extent, if any, is it willing to be bound to the prohibitions integral to this very *promise* or, for that matter, any promise at all?

The answer to these questions is the same as it was for Presidents Washington, Adams, Jefferson, Lincoln and perhaps, also, to the last president to have fully understood the contract fully, John Kennedy.

Yes, I'll cede the possibility that Ronald Reagan[61] did as well though I suspect his was more a function of his remarkable media presence and his skill in assigning anecdotal references. In either case, the answer to the question is this: Government has no such capability to comprehend a promise let alone interpret to what extent it will be bound. It is only by and through the vigilance of a tenacious and fully engaged people that government can be made to yield to their will. The temptations and allure of immense power are far too great to be permitted to operate solely on the thallic-like backbone whose concept of trust is viewed as on a temporary indulgence!

I invite you to continue this journey on to the two remaining volumes of this series. My commitment to the outcome lies in the promise that you will discover the means and methods by which, should it be our common resolve, to address these issues directly.

Still, I am reminded of a great many observations which before concluding this first and introductory volume are worth sharing. I will summarize them here, briefly, by simply recalling how I was so impressed by the common belief and kinship which existed between the people with whom I engaged in discourse and inquiry. The demeanor appeared in the form of a common identity that was neither Democrat-American, Republican-American etc., but simply as an American! I was impressed with this amazing sense of loyalty to the ideal of what *is* American and the desire to see it live and breathe. The desire to simultaneously be an individual and yet, at the same time, be whole and an integral part of *one!* It was palpable, pulsating to such a degree that it

---

61   My appearing to be less than deferential to President Reagan is only an appearance. I had the opportunity to meet him during a campaign event; a remarkable presence. His was a truly presidential form of executive leadership though to me, his depth of understanding of government dysfunction was not as tactile as JFK who, I admit, had the extraordinary advantage of RFK as his confidant and attorney general. Again, no offense intended, these are only my opinions.

was as if I could reach out and touch it and so, having this experience, I am ever more committed to its preservation. Nothing it would seem, could be more important. *Nothing!*

And so, let me leave you for now with the closing comments:

We cannot hope to change that which is shapeless nor can we claim to confine the ideals of providence such that they conform to our will. As in the case with the emotion we identify as love, I may not be able to see it, yet I know when it is present. As with the ideal that we identify as truth, I may not see it either though the consequence of its absence we all endure. I know not the form of faith; however, we know its outcome in practice and though I've no gauge with which I might measure character, one finds it a perfect companion along the path of its pursuit.

The principles worth knowing are not those that are seen, they are only those which accompany our most noble ideals and remain resolute as a witness to our success. They are not in the saying, they are *only* in the doing. It is for these reasons that there is no making right a wrong. There is no making a man rich by making a rich man poor. There is no advocating government as the cure for the unwilling by conscripting the resources of another; for the unworthy recipient will, in short order, only come to insist on what he/she has come to expect, not knowing or caring that government is not the cure but the culprit, the pathogen!

There is no claiming victory in failure unless it is in failure we claim the will to try again and again until we shape the courage required for victory. There is nothing gained by claiming equality if it is only accomplished by lowering the standard where true equality might rightly be attained. It is only through one's own genius that others are compelled to ascend, not by their lethargy. And there is no truth in the ideal of liberty if your concept of freedom is evidenced only by your willingness to purge that of another's.

No man will survive beyond the passage of time assigned to him and if for this reason only, we must all champion the same cause: The perfecting within each other a greater notion of what is most noble and commit to the pursuit of nothing less! In doing so we may yet find true allegiance with the silent call of providential ideals that we hold "to be self-evident" such that they are no longer just words but our practice; *no longer* an idle promise but as absolute as the passage of time. This notion might very well be our ultimate challenge, an enlightenment waiting patiently for its human companion. Failing this, we might very well suspend to a new and darker age!

> *"How soon the labor of men would make a paradise of the whole earth, were it not for misgovernment, and a diversion of all his energies from their proper object — the happiness of man — to the selfish interest of kings, nobles, and priests."* [62]

---

62   Thomas Jefferson: Letter to Ellen W. Coolidge, 1825. The context of the letter, however relevant to his communications with his Granddaughter (E.W. Coolidge), it keenly illustrates Mr. Jefferson's philosophical viewpoint as to the risks, by omission(s), of sound Governance.

Appendix: I

"Q & A"

I thought it would be a helpful companion for the material presented in *Blind Vision* to include a compilation of questions and my accompanying responses as they occurred over a series of months beginning in mid-2008. They appear in no particular order and though I assure you none of these were scripted, I was pleased to discover a consistency in their resolution. I truly hope you will find them interesting.

1.   What do you see as our country's greatest failure?

Prohibiting the expression of our highest ideals by allowing their construct, our representative form of government, to be weakened.

2.   What would you do to fix our Constitution?

The Constitution is self-regulating and needs only to be followed and applied with persistent resolve. In this, there is the perfection of its design. It, as an entity unto itself, neither needs nor requires fixing.

3.   Why are you so opposed to unions?

My message has been misinterpreted. I am not against unions; this country is a union. As unions are structured today they have become an institutionalized form of militancy. They have become a means to project the will of a few (which may also mean only a few in the union) and subsequently become a burden upon the whole. This is a soft form of fascism.

4. **I think your position on Social Security is wrong. We have a responsibility to take care of the elderly. Why are you so willing to ignore them?**

Good question. Unfortunately, your foundation is lost in your altruistic tendencies. Let me ask you this question: Who is the "we" you refer to and do they know you're speaking for them? How many 'elderly' are you personally actually taking care of? I never suggested we don't have a responsibility to one another. I do believe however, we have a greater responsibility and that is not to force others to become responsible for you and subject to your choices or your lack of making sound ones! Further, using government to impose altruism on me, or for that matter anyone else, is fascism. If we are going to be a fascist nation then we *all* should agree on the transition, not just the mob! At most, the government should help to facilitate individual planning for retirement self-reliance, not provide a life support system because someone has chosen not to.

5. **Much has been said about reintroducing the Fairness Doctrine. What are your thoughts on this?**

It's a frightening thought that a government of free people would even consider such a notion. A lively discourse is necessary in a free and just society; it permits the diversity of opinion to settle the contrivances that exist in all extremes. These ideas are fascist in nature as they seek not to benefit the free flow of ideas and information, but only to keep you from knowing that it is not occurring. It leaves the opposing point both anonymous and silent. By all means, it should be strongly opposed!

6. **How would you improve the presidential election process?**

Prohibit active legislators from being candidates and institute a four-year waiting period which would commence the day following their Senate or Congressional term. Consider the benefit of prohibiting party identity in the process. Require security screening prior to nomination. Prohibit campaign contributions of all kinds at best, U.S. Citizen (only) contributions however there should be strict monetary and annual limits occurring only in the election year of the specific office being voted upon. Establish campaign time limits. Establish a PBS-like media outlet active only in a designated *campaign season.* These are a few examples.

7. **Do you feel our government is broken?**

Yes and no. When I consider government as it is presently practiced however, the current relativism and politicization is not a function of the government construct, it is a function of how it is applied. For example, the game of baseball is played on the field, and the degree to which it is played by the rules that define the game it is also the degree to which it resembles the game of baseball. When the established structure of the game is no longer followed, its no longer the game of baseball; it becomes something entirely different.

8. **Religion has created many problems in man's history. Don't you think we should keep religion out of politics? You are aware, of course, that the Constitution requires separation of church and state?**

First, it is unfair to say religion is or has been a problem; it is intellectually benign at best. It is far more accurate to say that more often, throughout history, it has been man's expression of his opposition to moral and just practices that has been the problem. The Constitution mandates the prohibition of the state establishing or mandating a religion, not its prohibition. Equally important is the reality that it is not possible to separate religion, whatever form it is, from the individual; it's the equivalent of attempting to take the wet out of water. One's religion or moral compass, as it where, is what defines who the individual is. It is an indicator of how the individual will tack in the social interactions of his or her life. It defines the compass from which one not only perceive his role in life but also how and from what foundation or within what parameters he will function in the process.

9. **I gather you don't want government intervention in any part of an individual's life. But don't you think, in the case of gun ownership, that the dangers guns represent require the government to intervene?**

    A two-part question deserves a two-part answer. Yes, there is a role for government, but only to guard the very rights of the individual to own and possess any weapon she or he chooses. Yes, any weapon, and not to infringe upon said right. It is the action and its consequence that should be adjudicated, not the instrument of the action; a weapon is merely a tool that on its own has no means to perfect consequence. How then, can you reasonably restrict it? More people are killed with automobiles than with handguns — do you suggest we outlaw these too? How about knives? Swat teams actually kill more people than the alleged criminal they are targeting do! Do you then outlaw swat teams? A human thumb can be a more efficient tool of death than a pistol. Do we then outlaw thumbs? This type of logic appeals to anyone wanting to justify nearly any type of government action. If we permit the government to protect itself by disarming the people, who then is left to protect you?"

10. **What are your thoughts on national health care and how would you recommend the government handle the question?**

    Wow, a loaded question! First, let me reward your question by saying you'll find a complete answer to this question in volume three of the "Blind Vision" series, *Valor in Prosperity*. Next, to your question "How would I recommend the government...?" I would answer it this way: What has happened to our national conscience that we believe the government should be involved, at all, in the process? Haven't we sufficient evidence, yet, to see how the government is incapable of performing an economic function? Aren't the malignant failures of Lyndon Johnson's Great Society sufficient proof? (E.g., Social Security, Medicaid/ Medicare and the near countless other federal and state programs.) How can we sanely consider that more of a bad thing makes an already terrible situation better? However, there is a solution. For the idea to truly function, it cannot have the "economic crutch" of government involved with it. When the tensional forces that compel economic efficiency are removed (which is precisely what happens when government intervenes) then you no longer have the benefit of economic efficiency. To come to a sustainable solution regarding any government program we must first start with the addressing the fundamental flaw, as I just stated, that is inherent in all things government. I assure you, a profoundly functional way to address this issue exits.

11. You seem to have very strong opinions on religion and individual freedom. How do you reconcile these concepts with the rights of gay couples to get married?

I see no need to reconcile either of these with or within the construct of religion, or for that matter individual freedom particularly as it relates to government. I'm sorry I don't see the connection. See, the challenge of this, if I may call it a challenge, is largely the same for all other things the government participates in. It requires an entirely different paradigm be created, a whole new way of thinking for each new issue that some group wants to address through the construct we call government. I refer to this created paradigm as "Flat Earth Idolatry." As an example, government needs to regiment affirmative action, Social Security, or any entitlement program for that matter. The moment one takes on this discussion, in order to give it teeth, to give it "standing," a whole abstract series of presumed notions needs to be constructed and adopted and then (by agreement or by aggression) this new thinking superimposed above and/or over the prefix that exists – which, as I said, the government shouldn't be involved with in the first place. This pure lunacy exists because what you have is constantly changing paradigms, which then become no paradigm at all, just utter chaos. Now, to your question. Let me ask you this: Do you favor gay marriage? If so, then here's what you do: Accumulate a majority of people who feel the way you do and have a law passed that represents the "favored" position. That is representative democracy. The problem with the issue of gay marriage is that it approaches the issue (largely because the movement knows it cannot get a majority opinion) based on the crafting of their unique paradigm, their "Flat Earth Idolatry" that attempts to argue, in effect, what becomes fiat enforcement through court action. Which is to say the legal department will argue the case that gay marriage should not result on its merits but on the strength of distorting the applicability of the Fifth (due process) and the Fourteenth (equal protection) Amendments to the U.S. Constitution. It is indeed a "Flat Earth Idolatry" approach primarily because these two amendments were in direct response to government intrusions upon the inalienable rights of a sovereign individual — and not a social group. This is a very key point! Now, to illustrate just how key the point is: If we take the position that these two amendments are indeed relevant to the case and that they are given standing before the Court as sovereign individuals, much as blacks were (which gave rise, arguably, to the Fourteenth Amendment in the first place) and the Court resolves this argument in favor of the movement, then consider this: How then, would you address the rights of the majority who voted in opposition to the legislation prohibiting recognition of gay marriage? How would you address the same issue with respect to the government's outlawing polygamy? Not to mention any other group that could rally under the same proposition. The proof of the invalid nature of the argument is evidenced by these assertions and I have a sense that the group knows it; however, they are counting on the judicial weakness of the Court to favor their position.

APPENDIX: II

PRESIDENT GEORGE WASHINGTON'S
FAREWELL ADDRESS

SEPTEMBER 19TH, 1796

"Friends, & Fellow Citizens.

The period for a new election of a Citizen, to Administer the Executive government of the United States, being not far distant, and the time actually arrived, when your thoughts must be employed in designating the person, who is to be clothed with that important trust, it appears to me proper, especially as it may conduce to a more distinct expression of the public voice, that I should now apprise you of the resolution I have formed, to decline being considered among the number of those, out of whom a choice is to be made.

I beg you, at the same time, to do me the justice to be assured, that this resolution has not been taken, without a strict regard to all the considerations appertaining to the relation, which binds a dutiful Citizen to his country and that, in withdrawing the tender of service which silence in my Situation might imply, I am influenced by no diminution of zeal for your future interest, no deficiency of grateful respect for your past kindness; but am supported by a full conviction that the step is compatible with both.

The acceptance of, & continuance hitherto in, the Office to which your Suffrages have twice called me, have been a uniform sacrifice of inclination to the opinion of duty, and to a deference for what appeared to be your desire. I constantly hoped, that it would have been much earlier in my power, consistently with motives, which I was not at liberty to disregard, to return to that retirement, from which I had been reluctantly drawn. The strength of my inclination to do this, previous to the last Election, had even led to the preparation of an address to declare it to you; but mature reflection on the then perplexed & critical posture of our Affairs with foreign nations, and the unanimous advice of persons entitled to my confidence, impelled me to abandon the idea.

I rejoice, that the state of your concerns, external as well as internal, no longer renders the pursuit of inclination incompatible with the sentiment of duty, or propriety; and am persuaded whatever partiality may be retained for my services, that in the present circumstances of our country, you will not disapprove my determination to retire.

The impressions, with which, I first undertook the arduous trust, were explained on the proper occasion. In the discharge of this trust, I will only say, that I have, with good intentions, contributed towards the Organization and Administration of the government, the best exertions of which a very fallible judgment was capable. Not unconscious, in the outset, of the inferiority of my qualifications, experience in my own eyes, perhaps still more in the eyes of others, has strengthened the motives to diffidence of myself; and every day the increasing weight of years admonishes me more and more, that the shade of retirement is as necessary to me as it will be welcome. *Satisfied that if any circumstances have given peculiar value to my services, they were temporary, I have the consolation to believe, that while choice and prudence invite me to quit the political scene, patriotism does not forbid it.*

In looking forward to the moment, which is intended to terminate the career of my public life, my feelings do not permit me to suspend the deep acknowledgment of that debt of gratitude which I owe to my beloved country, for the many honors it has conferred upon me; still more for the steadfast confidence with which it has supported me; and for the opportunities I have thence enjoyed of manifesting my inviolable attachment, by services faithful & persevering, though in usefulness unequal to my zeal. If benefits have resulted to our country from these services, let it always be remembered to your praise, and as an instructive example in our annals, that, under circumstances in which the Passions agitated in every direction were liable to mislead, amidst appearances sometimes dubious, vicissitudes of fortune often discouraging, in situations in which not unfrequently want of Success has countenanced the spirit of criticism, the constancy of your support was the essential prop of the efforts, and a guarantee of the plans by which they were effected. Profoundly penetrated with this idea, I shall carry it with me to my grave, as a strong incitement to unceasing vows that Heaven may continue to you the choicest tokens of its beneficence that your Union & brotherly affection may be perpetual—that the free constitution, which is the work of your hands, may be sacredly maintained—that its Administration in every department may be stamped with wisdom and Virtue—that, in fine, the happiness of the people of these States, under the auspices of liberty, may be made complete, by so careful a preservation and so prudent a use of this blessing as will acquire to them the glory of recommending it to the applause, the affection—and adoption of every nation which is yet a stranger to it.

Here, perhaps, I ought to stop. But a solicitude for your welfare, which cannot end but with my life, and the apprehension of danger, natural to that solicitude, urge me on an occasion like the present, to offer to your solemn contemplation, and to recommend to your frequent review, some sentiments; which are the result of much reflection, of no inconsiderable observation, and which appear to me all important to the permanency of your felicity as a People. These will be offered to you with the more freedom as you can only see in them the disinterested warnings of a parting friend, who can possibly have no personal motive to bias his counsel. Nor can I forget, as an encouragement to it, your indulgent reception of my sentiments on a former and not dissimilar occasion. Interwoven as is the love of liberty with every ligament of your hearts, no recommendation of mine is necessary to fortify or confirm the Attachment.

The Unity of Government which constitutes you one people is also now dear to you. It is justly so; for it is a main Pillar in the Edifice of your real independence, the support of your tranquility at home; your peace abroad; of your safety; of your prosperity; of that very Liberty which you so highly prize. But as it is easy to foresee, that from different causes & from different quarters, much pains will be taken, many artifices employed, to weaken in your minds the conviction of this truth; as this is the point in your political fortress against which the batteries of internal & external enemies will be most constantly and actively (though often covertly & insidiously) directed, it is of infinite moment, that you should properly estimate the immense value of your national Union to your collective & individual happiness; that you should cherish a cordial, habitual & immoveable attachment to it; accustoming yourselves to think and speak of it as of the Palladium of your political safety and prosperity; watching for its preservation with jealous anxiety; discountenancing whatever may suggest even a suspicion that it can in any event be abandoned, and indignantly frowning upon the first *dawning of every attempt to alienate any portion of our Country from the rest, or to enfeeble the sacred ties which now link together the various parts.*

For this you have every inducement of sympathy and interest. Citizens by birth or choice, of a common country, that country has a right to concentrate your affections. The name of American, which belongs to you, in your national capacity, must always exalt the just pride of Patriotism, more than any appellation derived from local discriminations.

With slight shades of difference, you have the same Religion, Manners, Habits & political Principles. You have in a common cause fought & triumphed together. The independence & liberty you possess are the work of joint councils, and joint efforts of common dangers, sufferings and successes.

But these considerations, however powerfully they address themselves to your sensibility are greatly outweighed by those which apply more immediately to your Interest. Here every portion of our country finds the most commanding motives for carefully guarding & preserving the Union of the whole.

The North, in an unrestrained intercourse with the South, protected by the equal Laws of a common government, finds in the productions of the latter, great additional resources of Maritime & commercial enterprise and—precious materials of manufacturing industry. The South in the same Intercourse, benefiting by the Agency of the North, sees its agriculture grow & its commerce expand. Turning partly into its own channels the seamen of the North, it finds its particular navigation invigorated; and while it contributes, in different ways, to nourish & increase the general mass of the National navigation, it looks forward to the protection of a Maritime strength, to which itself is unequally adapted. The East, in a like intercourse with the West, already finds, and in the progressive improvement of interior communications, by land & water, will more & more find a valuable vent for the commodities which it brings from abroad, or manufactures at home. The West derives from the East supplies requisite to its growth & comfort and what is perhaps of still greater consequence, it must of necessity owe the Secure enjoyment of indispensable outlets for its own productions to the weight, influence, and the future maritime strength of the Atlantic side of the Union, directed by an indissoluble community of Interest as one Nation. Any other tenure by which the West can hold this essential advantage, whether derived from its own separate strength, or from an apostate & unnatural connection with any foreign Power, must be intrinsically precarious.

While then every part of our country thus feels an immediate & particular Interest in Union, all the parts combined cannot fail to find in the united mass of means & efforts greater strength, greater resource, proportionably greater security from external danger, a less frequent interruption of their Peace by foreign Nations; and, what is of inestimable value! they must derive from Union an exemption from those broils and Wars between themselves, which

so frequently afflict neighboring countries, not tied together by the same government; which their own rivalships alone would be sufficient to produce, but which opposite foreign alliances, attachments & intrigues would stimulate & embitter. Hence likewise they will avoid the necessity of those overgrown Military establishments, which under any form of Government are inauspicious to liberty, and which are to be regarded as particularly hostile to Republican Liberty: In this sense it is, that your union ought to be considered as a main prop of your liberty, and that the love of the one ought to endear to you the preservation of the other.

These considerations speak a persuasive language to every reflecting & virtuous mind, and exhibit the continuance of the Union as a primary object of Patriotic desire. Is there a doubt, whether a common government can embrace so large a sphere? Let experience solve it. To listen to mere speculation in such a case were criminal. We are authorized to hope that a proper organization of the whole, with the auxiliary agency of governments for the respective Subdivisions, will afford a happy issue to the experiment. 'Tis well worth a fair and full experiment.

With such powerful and obvious motives to Union, affecting all parts of our country, while experience shall not have demonstrated its impracticability, there will always be reason, to distrust the patriotism of those, who in any quarter may endeavor to weaken its bands.

In contemplating the causes which may disturb our Union, it occurs as matter of serious concern, that any ground should have been furnished for characterizing parties by Geographical discriminations, Northern and Southern, Atlantic and Western; whence designing men may endeavor to excite a belief that there is a real difference of local interests and views.

One of the expedients of Party to acquire influence, within particular districts, is to misrepresent the opinions & aims of other Districts. You cannot shield yourselves too much against the jealousies & heart burnings which spring from these misrepresentations. They tend to render Alien to each other those who ought to be bound together by fraternal Affection. The Inhabitants of our Western country have lately had a useful lesson on this head. They have Seen, in the Negotiation by the Executive, and in the unanimous ratification by the Senate, of the Treaty with Spain, and in the universal satisfaction at that event, throughout the United States, a decisive proof how unfounded were the suspicions propagated among them of a policy in the General Government and in the Atlantic States unfriendly to their Interests in regard to the Mississippi. They have been witnesses to the formation of two Treaties, that with G: Britain and that with Spain, which secure to them every thing they could desire, in respect to our Foreign relations, towards confirming their prosperity. Will it not be their wisdom to rely for the preservation of these advantages on the Union by which they were procured? Will they not henceforth be deaf to those Advisers, if such there are, who would sever them from their Brethren and connect them with Aliens?

To the efficacy and permanency of Your Union, a Government for the whole is indispensable. No Alliances however strict between the parts can be an adequate substitute. They must inevitably experience the infractions & interruptions which all Alliances in all times have experienced. Sensible of this momentous truth, you have improved upon your first essay, by the adoption of a Constitution of Government, better calculated than your former for an intimate Union, and for the efficacious management of your common concerns. This government, the offspring of our own choice uninfluenced and unawed, adopted upon full investigation & mature deliberation, completely free in its principles, in the distribution of its powers, uniting security with energy, and containing within itself a provision for its own amendment, has a just claim to your confidence and your support. Respect for its authority, compliance with its Laws, acquiescence in its measures, are duties enjoined by the fundamental maxims of true Liberty. The basis of our political Systems is the right of the people to make and to alter their Constitutions of Government. But the Constitution which at any time exists, 'till changed by an explicit and authentic act of the whole People, is sacredly obligatory upon all. The very idea of the power and the right of the People to establish Government presupposes the duty of every Individual to obey the established Government.

All obstructions to the execution of the Laws, all combinations and Associations, under whatever plausible character, with the real design to direct,

control counteract, or awe the regular deliberation and action of the Con-
stituted authorities are destructive of this fundamental principle and of
fatal tendency. They serve to Organize faction, to give it an artificial and
extraordinary force—to put in the place of the delegated will of the Nation,
the will of a party; often a small but artful and enterising minority of the
Community; and, according to the alternate triumphs of different parties,
to make the public Administration the Mirror of the ill concerted and
incongruous projects of faction, rather than the Organ of consistent and
wholesome plans digested by common councils and modified by mutual
interests. However combinations or Associations of the above description
may now & then answer popular ends, they are likely, in the course of time
and things, to become potent engines, by which cunning, ambitious and
unprincipled men will be enabled to subvert the Power of the People, &
to usurp for themselves the reins of Government; destroying afterwards the
very engines which have lifted them to unjust dominion.

Towards the preservation of your Government and the permanency of your
present happy state, it is requisite, not only that you steadily discountenance
irregular oppositions to its acknowledged authority, but also that you resist
with care the spirit of innovation upon its principles however specious the
pretexts. One method of assault may be to effect, in the forms of the Consti-
tution, alterations which will impair the energy of the system, and thus to
undermine what cannot be directly overthrown. In all the changes to which
you may be invited, remember that time and habit are at least as necessary
to fix the true character of Governments, as of other human institutions
that experience is the surest standard, by which to test the real tendency of
the existing Constitution of a Country, that facility in changes upon the
credit of mere hypotheses & opinion exposes to perpetual change, from the
endless variety of hypotheses and opinion: and remember, especially, that
for the efficient management of your common interests, in a country so

extensive as ours, a Government of as much vigor as is consistent with the perfect security of Liberty is indispensable; Liberty itself will find in such a Government, with powers properly distributed and adjusted, its surest Guardian. It is indeed little else than a name, where the Government is too feeble to withstand the enterprises of faction, to confine each member of the Society within the limits prescribed by the laws & to maintain all in the secure & tranquil enjoyment of the rights of person & property.

I have already intimated to you the danger of Parties in the State, with particular reference to the founding of them on Geographical discriminations. Let me now take a more comprehensive view, & warn you in the most solemn manner against the baneful effects of the Spirit of Party, generally.

This Spirit, unfortunately, is inseparable from our nature, having its root in the strongest passions of the human Mind. It exists under different shapes in all Governments, more or less stifled, controlled, or repressed; but in those of the popular form it is seen in its greatest rankness and is truly their worst enemy.

The alternate domination of one faction over another, sharpened by the spirit of revenge natural to party dissention, which in different ages & countries has perpetrated the most horrid enormities, is itself a frightful despotism. But this leads at length to a more formal and permanent despotism. The disorders & miseries, which result, gradually incline the minds of men to seek security & repose in the absolute power of an Individual: and sooner or later the chief of some prevailing faction more able or more fortunate than his competitors, turns this disposition to the purposes of his own elevation, on the ruins of Public Liberty.

Without looking forward to an extremity of this kind (which nevertheless ought not to be entirely out of sight) the common & continual mischiefs of the spirit of Party are sufficient to make it the interest and the duty of a wise People to discourage and restrain it

It serves always to distract the Public Councils and enfeeble the Public Administration. It agitates the Community with ill founded Jealousies and false alarms, kindles the animosity of one part against another, foments occasionally riot & insurrection. It opens the door to foreign influence & corruption, which find a facilitated access to the government itself through the channels of party passions. Thus the policy and the will of one country, are subjected to the policy and will of another.

There is an opinion that parties in free countries are useful checks upon the Administration of the Government and serve to keep alive the spirit of Liberty. This within certain limits is probably true and in Governments of a Monarchical cast Patriotism may look with indulgence, if not with favor, upon the spirit of party. But in those of the popular character, in Governments purely elective, it is a spirit not to be encouraged. From their natural tendency, it is certain there will always be enough of that spirit for every salutary purpose. And there being constant danger of excess, the effort ought to be, by force of public opinion, to mitigate & assuage it. A fire not to be quenched; it demands a uniform vigilance to prevent its bursting into a flame, lest instead of warming it should consume.

It is important, likewise, that the habits of thinking in a free Country should inspire caution in those entrusted with its Administration, to confine themselves within their respective Constitutional Spheres; avoiding in the exercise of the Powers of one department to encroach upon another. The spirit of encroachment tends to consolidate the powers of all the departments in one, and thus to create whatever the form of government, a real despotism. A just estimate of that love of power, and proneness to abuse it, which predominates in the human heart, is sufficient to satisfy us of the truth of this position. *The necessity of reciprocal checks in the exercise of political power; by dividing and distributing it into different depositories, & constituting each the Guardian of the Public Weal against invasions by the others, has been evinced by experiments ancient & modern; some of them in our country & under our own eyes. To preserve them must be as necessary as to institute them. If in the opinion of the People, the distribution or modification of the Constitutional powers be in any particular wrong, let it be corrected by an amendment in the way which the Constitution designates. But let there be no change by usurpation; for though this, in one instance, may be the instrument of good, it is the customary weapon by which free governments are destroyed. The precedent must always greatly overbalance in permanent evil any partial or transient benefit which the use can at any time yield.*

Of all the dispositions and habits which lead to political prosperity, Religion and morality are indispensable supports. In vain would that man claim the tribute of Patriotism, who should labor to subvert these great Pillars of human happiness, these firmest props of the duties of Men & citizens. The mere Politician, equally with the pious man ought to respect & to cherish them. A volume could not trace all their connections with private & public felicity. Let it simply be asked where is the security for property, for reputation, for life, if the sense of religious obligation desert the Oaths, which are the instruments of investigation in Courts of Justice? And let us with caution indulge the supposition, that morality can be maintained without religion. Whatever may be conceded to the influence of refined education on minds of peculiar structure—reason & experience both forbid us to expect that National morality can prevail in exclusion of religious principle.

'Tis substantially true, that virtue or morality is a necessary spring of popular government. The rule indeed extends with more or less force to

every species of Free Government. Who that is a sincere friend to it, can look with indifference upon attempts to shake the foundation of the fabric.

Promote then as an object of primary importance, Institutions for the general diffusion of knowledge. In proportion as the structure of a government gives force to public opinion, it is essential that public opinion should be enlightened.

As a very important source of strength & security, cherish public credit. One method of preserving it is to use it as sparingly as possible: avoiding occasions of expense by cultivating peace, but remembering also that timely disbursements to prepare for danger frequently prevent much greater disbursements to repel it, avoiding likewise the accumulation of debt, not only by shunning occasions of expense, but by vigorous exertions in time of Peace to discharge the Debts which unavoidable wars may have occasioned, not ungenerously throwing upon posterity the burthen which we ourselves ought to bear. The execution of these maxims belongs to your Representatives, but it is necessary that public opinion should cooperate. To facilitate to them the performance of their duty, it is essential that you should practically bear in mind, that towards the payment of debts there must be Revenue (that to have Revenue there must be taxes) that no taxes can be devised which are not more or less inconvenient & unpleasant that the intrinsic embarrassment inseparable from the Selection of the proper objects (which is always a choice of difficulties) ought to be a decisive motive for a candid construction of the Conduct of the Government in making it, and for a spirit of acquiescence in the measures for obtaining Revenue which the public exigencies may at any time dictate.

Observe good faith & justice towards all Nations. Cultivate peace & harmony with all. Religion & morality enjoin this conduct; and can it be that good policy does not equally enjoin it? It will be worthy of a free, enlightened, and, at no distant period, a great Nation, to give to mankind the magnanimous and too novel example of a People always guided by an exalted justice & benevolence. Who can doubt that in the course of time and things the fruits of such a plan would richly repay any temporary advantages which might be lost by a steady adherence to it? Can it be, that Providence has not connected the permanent felicity of a Nation with its virtue? The experiment, at least, is recommended by every sentiment which ennobles human Nature. Alas! Is it rendered impossible by its vices?

In the execution of such a plan nothing is more essential than that permanent inveterate antipathies against particular Nations and passionate attachments for others should be excluded; and that in place of them just & amicable feelings towards all should be cultivated. The Nation, which indulges towards another an habitual hatred, or an habitual fondness, is in some degree a slave. It is a slave to its animosity or to its affection, either of which is sufficient to lead it astray from its duty and its interest. Antipathy in one Nation against another disposes each more readily to offer insult and injury, to lay hold of slight causes of umbrage, and to be haughty and intractable, when accidental or trifling occasions of dispute occur. Hence frequent collisions, obstinate envenomed and bloody contests. The Nation, prompted by ill will & resentment sometimes impels to War the Government, contrary to the best calculations of policy. The Government sometimes participates in the national propensity, and adopts through passion what reason would reject; at other times, it makes the animosity of the Nation subservient to projects of hostility instigated by pride, ambition and other sinister & pernicious motives. The peace often, sometimes perhaps the Liberty, of Nations has been the victim.

So likewise, a passionate attachment of one Nation for another produces a variety of evils. Sympathy for the favorite nation, facilitating the illusion of an imaginary common interest, in cases where no real common interest exists, and infusing into one the enmities of the other, betrays the former into a participation in the quarrels & Wars of the latter, without adequate inducement or justification: It leads also to concessions to the favorite Nation of privileges denied to others, which is apt doubly to injure the Nation making the concessions, by unnecessarily parting with what ought to have been retained, and by exciting jealousy, ill will, and a disposition to retaliate, in the parties from whom equal privileges are withheld: And it gives to ambitious, corrupted, or deluded citizens (who devote themselves to the favorite Nation) facility to betray, or sacrifice the interests of their own country, without odium, sometimes even with popularity; gilding with the appearances of a virtuous sense of obligation a commendable deference for public opinion, or a laudable zeal for public good, the base or foolish compliances of ambition corruption or infatuation.

As avenues to foreign influence in innumerable ways, such attachments are particularly alarming to the truly enlightened and independent Patriot. How many opportunities do they afford to tamper with domestic factions, to practice the arts of seduction, to mislead public opinion, to influence or awe the public Councils! Such an attachment of a small or weak, towards a great & powerful Nation, dooms the former to be the satellite of the latter.

Against the insidious wiles of foreign influence, (I conjure you to believe me fellow citizens,), the jealousy of a free people ought to be constantly awake; since history and experience prove that foreign influence is one of the most baneful foes of Republican Government. But that jealousy to be useful must be impartial; else it becomes the instrument of the very influence to be avoided, instead of a defense against it. Excessive partiality for one foreign nation and excessive dislike of another, cause those whom they actuate to see danger only on one side, and serve to veil and even second the arts of influence on the other. Real Patriots, who may resist the intrigues of the favorite, are liable to become suspected and odious; while its tools and dupes usurp the applause & confidence of the people, to surrender their interests.

The Great rule of conduct for us, in regard to foreign Nations is in extending our commercial relations to have with them as little political connection as possible. So far as we have already formed engagements let them be fulfilled, with perfect good faith. Here let us stop.

Europe has a set of primary interests, which to us have none, or a very remote relation. Hence she must be engaged in frequent controversies, the causes of which are essentially foreign to our concerns. Hence therefore it must be unwise in us to implicate ourselves, by artificial ties, in the ordinary vicissitudes of her politics, or the ordinary combinations & collisions of her friendships, or enmities.

Our detached & distant situation invites and enables us to pursue a different course. If we remain one People, under an efficient government, the period is not far off, when we may defy material injury from external annoyance; when we may take such an attitude as will cause the neutrality we may at any time resolve upon to be scrupulously respected; when belligerent nations, under the impossibility of making acquisitions upon us, will not lightly hazard the giving us provocation; when we may choose peace or War, as our interest guided by justice shall Counsel.

Why forego the advantages of so peculiar a situation? Why quit our own to stand upon foreign ground? Why, by interweaving our destiny with that of any part of Europe, entangle our peace and prosperity in the toils of European Ambition, Rivalship, Interest, Humor or Caprice?

'Tis our true policy to steer clear of permanent Alliances, with any portion of the foreign World—So far, I mean, as we are now at liberty to do it, for let me not be understood as capable of patronizing infidelity to existing engagements, (I hold the maxim no less applicable to public than to private affairs, that honesty is always the best policy) I repeat it therefore, Let those engagements. be observed in their genuine sense. But in my opinion, it is unnecessary and would be unwise to extend them. Taking care always to keep ourselves, by suitable establishments, on a respectably defensive posture, we may safely trust to temporary alliances for extraordinary emergencies.

Harmony, liberal intercourse with all Nations, are recommended by policy, humanity and interest. But even our Commercial policy should hold an equal and impartial hand: neither seeking nor granting exclusive favors or preferences; consulting the natural course of things; diffusing & diversifying by gentle means the streams of Commerce, but forcing nothing; establishing with Powers so disposed in order to give to trade a stable course, to define the rights of our Merchants, and to enable the Government to support them—conventional rules of intercourse;

the best that present circumstances and mutual opinion will permit, but temporary, & liable to be from time to time abandoned or varied, as experience and circumstances shall dictate; constantly keeping in view, that 'tis folly in one Nation to look for disinterested favors from another, that it must pay with a portion of its Independence for whatever it may accept under that character, that by such acceptance, it may place itself in the condition of having given equivalents for nominal favors and yet of being reproached with ingratitude for not giving more. There can be no greater error than to expect, or calculate upon real favors from Nation to Nation. 'Tis an illusion which experience must cure, which a just pride ought to discard.

In offering to you, my Countrymen, these counsels of an old and affectionate friend, I dare not hope they will make the strong and lasting impression, I could wish that they will control the usual current of the passions, or prevent our Nation from running the course which has hitherto marked the Destiny of Nations: But if I may even flatter myself, that they may be productive of some partial benefit, some occasional good; that they may now and then recur to moderate the fury of party spirit, to warn against the mischiefs of foreign Intrigue, to guard against the Impostures of pretended patriotism—this hope will be a full recompense for the solicitude for your welfare, by which they have been dictated. How far in the discharge of my Official duties, I have been guided by the principles which have been delineated, the public Records and other evidences of my conduct must witness to You and to the world. To myself, the assurance of my own conscience is, that I have at least believed myself to be guided by them.

In relation to the still subsisting War in Europe, my Proclamation of the 22d of April 1793 is the index to my Plan. Sanctioned by your approving voice and by that of Your Representatives in both Houses of Congress, the spirit of that measure has continually governed me; uninfluenced by any attempts to deter or divert me from it.

After deliberate examination with the aid of the best lights I could obtain I was well satisfied that our Country, under all the circumstances of the case, had a right to take, and was bound in duty and interest, to take a Neutral position. Having taken it, I determined, as far as should depend upon me, to maintain it, with moderation, perseverance & firmness

The considerations, which respect the right to hold this conduct, it is not necessary on this occasion to detail. I will only observe, that according to my understanding of the matter, that right, so far from being denied by any of the Belligerent Powers has been virtually admitted by all.

The duty of holding a neutral conduct may be inferred, without any thing more, from the obligation which justice and humanity impose on every Nation, in cases in which it is free to act, to maintain inviolate the relations of Peace and amity towards other Nations. The inducements of interest for observing that conduct will best be referred to your own reflections & experience. With me, a predominant motive has been to endeavor to gain time to our country to settle & mature its yet recent institutions, and to progress without interruption, to that degree of strength & consistency, which is necessary to give it, humanly speaking, the command of its own fortunes.

Though in reviewing the incidents of my Administration, I am unconscious of intentional error—I am nevertheless too sensible of my defects not to think it probable that I may have committed many errors. Whatever they may be I fervently beseech the Almighty to avert or mitigate the evils to which they may tend. I shall also carry with me the hope that my Country will never cease to view them with indulgence; and that after forty five years of my life dedicated to its Service, with an upright zeal, the faults of incompetent abilities will be consigned to oblivion, as myself must soon be to the Mansions of rest.

Relying on its kindness in this as in other things, and actuated by that fervent love towards it, which is so natural to a Man, who views in it the native soil of himself and his progenitors for several Generations; I anticipate with pleasing expectation that retreat, in which I promise myself to realize, without alloy, the sweet enjoyment of partaking, in the midst of my fellow Citizens, the benign influence of good Laws under a free Government—the ever favorite object of my heart, and the happy reward, as I trust, of our mutual cares, labors and dangers."

G. Washington

THE IMPERFECT MESSENGER™

FOUNDATION

On Point • On Purpose • In Practice

Presents:

Blind Vision

Series

VOLUME I:

We Hold These Truths...

VOLUME II:

Value Given, Value Received

VOLUME III:

Valor in Prosperity

VISIT US AT:

www.theimperfectmessenger.com

FACEBOOK:

www.theimperfectmessenger.com/facebook

TWITTER:

imprfctmsngr

TreeNeutral

Advantage Media Group is proud to be a part of the Tree Neutral™ program. Tree Neutral offsets the number of trees consumed in the production and printing of this book by taking proactive steps such as planting trees in direct proportion to the number of trees used to print books. To learn more about Tree Neutral, please visit **www.treeneutral. com.** To learn more about Advantage Media Group's commitment to being a responsible steward of the environment, please visit **www. advantagefamily.com/green**

We Hold These Truths... is available in bulk quantities at special discounts for corporate, institutional, and educational purposes. To learn more about the special programs Advantage Media Group offers, please visit **www.KaizenUniversity.com** or call 1.866.775.1696.

Advantage Media Group is a leading publisher of business, motivation, and self-help authors. Do you have a manuscript or book idea that you would like to have considered for publication? Please visit **www.amgbook.com**